PRAISE

"Laura Formentini has written a lovely book of life lessons through stories, poems, and vignettes of insight and wisdom and revelation. The ultimate result is reinventing life through conscious awareness of life's daily miracles of healing transformation and liberation. I highly recommend it."

–Deepak Chopra

"Turning the pain that grief leaves behind into a piece of beauty that lifts up others, Laura Formentini shares the life lessons that loving and losing her son has taught her in *Twentyone Olive Trees*. These tender and touching fables offer a message of hope to the grieving - that love never dies."

–Lindsey M. Henke, MSW,
LICSW Founder of Pregnancy After Loss Support

"*Twentyone Olive Trees* by Laura Formentini truly captured my heart. As a mom who has battled grief with the loss of my own son, I found Laura's poems to bring comfort and understanding - and her stories to bring a sense of calmness and connection. Fiction stories are such a wonderful way to offer healing - bringing the reader on a journey to safely feel emotions and offer growth along the way. *Twentyone Olive Trees* gives you this experience in such a beautiful way. I highly recommend!"

–Lindsay Gibson, Author of *Just Be: How My Stillborn Son Taught Me to Surrender*

"Inspiring and transformational......*Twentyone Olive Trees* illustrates the emotional journey of a mother's heart from deep grief to soulful healing offering a powerful and insightful perspective of mindfulness and new beginnings. Experiencing the loss of a child at any age, forever alters a parent's life. Beautifully and creatively illustrated and written, Laura's fables and poems entwine unique heartfelt lessons of love and reflective truths providing hope when it seems all is lost. A must read for grieving hearts...."

–Daphne Bach Greer, Author of *Barely Breathing: Ten Secrets to Surviving Loss of Your Child* and blogger at *The Sweeter Side of Grief.*

"Truly, *Twentyone Olive Trees* is a beautiful expression of a mother's aching love and will resonate with those who have experienced grief."

—**MEA SMITH,** *Grief Like a River: Poems and Illustrations*

"This is not your average book on grief and loss. Filled with hope and encouragement, Laura's beautiful fables, poems, and letters to her son, accompanied by absolutely gorgeous full color illustrations, left me feeling encouraged and uplifted. There are so many books that are instructional in nature, or recounts of personal events, or even advice on what to do through your grief, but this is nothing like that. It's an intriguing and uplifting book. I highly recommend it to anyone who is searching to heal after the loss of a child or loved one."

—**ALEXA BIGWARFE**, author, *Sunshine After the Storm: A Survival Guide for the Grieving Mother.*

"*Twentyone Olive Trees* is a tender invitation to fully embrace life and it's mysteries. Through fables and personal reflection, Laura Formentini integrates grief with unfaltering love. Amidst longing for her son, Laura gently reminds us we are always in connection to those we love and even through loss we are capable of growth."

—**AMIE LANDS**, author of *Navigating the Unknown & Perfectly Imperfect Family*

"The thread that runs through *Twentyone Olive Trees* is her eternal love for her son. As a grief counselor to parents who lose babies, I have witnessed countless times how the pain of the loss continues to transform over time and how much solace parents find when they eventually create an 'intuitive bridge' between themselves and their child, as the author did. The poignant poems beautifully express the varied experiences of bereaved parents, and the beautifully illustrated fables will teach children and adults alike important lessons in coping with grief and moving toward hope, acceptance and growth. The author's wish to 'lift up as many people as possible' will most certainly be realized as they use their own inner wisdom and imagination to connect with their child after death."

—**PASCALE VERMONT, PhD**, author of *Surviving the Unimaginable: Stories of Coping with Pregnancy and Infancy Loss*

TWENTYONE
Olive
Trees

TWENTYONE
Olive Trees

A mother's walk through
the grief of suicide to
hope and healing

Laura Formentini

KAT BIGGIE PRESS
Columbia, SC

Copyright © 2021 Laura Formentini

All rights reserved. No part of this book may be reproduced or transmitted in any form or by any means, electronic or mechanical, including photocopying, recording or by an information storage and retrieval system – except by a reviewer who may quote brief passages in a review to be printed in a magazine, newspaper or on the Web – without permission in writing from the publisher.

Published by Kat Biggie Press
www.Katbiggiepress.com

Illustrations by Marit Cooper
www.maritcooper.com

Design by Margaret Cogswell
www.margaretcogswell.com

Library of Congress Control Number: 2021914027

Publisher's Cataloging-In-Publication Data
(Prepared by The Donohue Group, Inc.)

Names: Formentini, Laura, author. | Cooper, Marit, illustrator.
Title: Twentyone olive trees : a mother's walk through the grief of
    suicide to hope and healing / by Laura Formentini ; [illustrated by
    Marit Cooper].
Other Titles: 21 olive trees
Description: First edition. | [Columbia, South Carolina] : Kat Biggie
    Press, [2022]
Identifiers: ISBN 9781955119061 (paperback) | ISBN 9781955119078
    (hardback) | ISBN 9781955119054 (ebook)
Subjects: LCSH: Formentini, Laura--Family--Anecdotes. | Parental grief--
    Anecdotes. | Children--Death--Psychological aspects--Anecdotes.|
    Suicide--Psychological aspects--Anecdotes. | LCGFT: Fables. | Poetry. |
    Anecdotes.
Classification: LCC BF575.G7 F67 2022 (print) | LCC BF575.G7 (ebook) | DDC
    155.937085--dc23

First edition

TABLE OF CONTENTS

I celebrate myself, and sing myself,
And what I assume you shall assume,
For every atom belonging to me as good
belongs to you

WALT WHITMAN

FOR BLAISE

Because ours is a fable woven
into a celestial garden

INTRODUCTION

Why this Book?
Because a soul mate connection never dies

This book, *Twentyone Olive Trees: A Mother's Walk through the Grief of Suicide to Hope and Healing,* is my personal journey of transformation following my son Blaise's suicide. The book traces my path from grief to understanding and healing, shown through a collection of twenty-one letters and poems I wrote to Blaise in the year after his untimely death. Before each of the letters, is a fable narrative I wrote. The morals of each story reflect the wisdom Blaise and I gained during the years we spent living and traveling together. The fables take a playful, childlike, and intimate look at coping with loss and embracing acceptance that I hope will intrigue, inspire, give hope, and offer ways for readers to transform their own personal loss and pain into something beautiful. The title takes its name from the twenty-one olive trees, one for each year of Blaise's life, that I will plant at a healing center I am currently creating in his honor. The olive tree is a symbol that reflects all the things about him, including peace, wisdom, immortality and regeneration.

My son Blaise was my soul mate and my partner in crime on many adventures. We lived together on two different continents and traveled seemingly everywhere around the world together, often to remote areas like Lapland in the northernmost region of Finland or the pyramids of Egypt. All the while, we had amazing and profound conversations about concepts like wisdom and folly, ate the craziest foods like scorpions on a stick in Cambodia, encouraged each other when we were afraid, and had as many moments of laughter and eccentricity as we did of confrontation. He was an incredibly sweet, generous, and ultra-sensitive soul. We had even planned to work together in the nonprofit field. I, as a philanthropist, would fundraise and tell stories through the documentaries he would create as a director. Because of our profound connection, it seemed like we'd both found our passions and shared the same enthusiasm for them.

However, Blaise was also an empath. Empaths are known for absorbing energy from people and places, the good and the bad, and to not be able to distinguish where their own emotions end and the other person's begin. His highly sensitive soul couldn't handle the harshness of the world in which he lived. Unfortunately, because of these pressures and a drug addiction that I didn't recognize, Blaise decided to take his own life. He left before realizing that his empathy was a gift. Empathy can heal. Empathy can bring about the changes that our society is so strongly in need of.

I have never, ever experienced the same amazing bond that I had with Blaise with anyone else in my life. In fact, the bond between Blaise and I has grown stronger, thanks to the great flow of energy that I feel still exists between us. Our soul mate relationship continues to this day, as he acts as my muse to bring healing transformation into the world.

Breathing New Life into the Transformation

Experiencing the loss of a dear loved one transforms what you thought their life was about. Even though their life can never be restored, it is in your power to create lasting change in their honor and breathe new life into their memory. Even the simple act of planting one tree can make a difference—and one day, a person may sit in the shade of that tree, thanks to your choosing not to give into your pain. It is my experience that transforming my pain in this positive way brought me back "home" in a spiritual sense.

Everything in nature transforms. We all belong to that constant natural process of change, including birth, death, and rebirth. Doesn't the butterfly leave its chrysalis to take to the air on its new wings? Doesn't the barred owl roost in its majestic nest, only to leave it after nesting season is over? Doesn't transformation always include a next phase?

We all transform, eventually. We all do. **No one gets out of life alive.** This wisdom became clear to me after a few months of painful, unbearable grieving, filled with wild mood swings—up and down, and then back up, sideways, and back down again. And all of that began the minute I was notified that my son Blaise had taken his life. I was in the highlands of Ethiopia, capturing stories of positive transformation when I received the news. After receiving that call, I cut short my trip in Africa. My wild mood swings continued as I traveled back to the US and then to Italy, fundraised for various causes, wrote my memoirs, and helped my other son buy a house.

At the time, I cried and cried, and I just wanted to sleep, and then I wanted to sleep some more. Repeat. This cycle continued until I eventually came to my breakthrough moment—when I realized what was really going on, I finally found my peace. I realized life is about evolution. You may have this moment too. The moment you realize you won't see that face anymore, you won't hear that laugh anymore, and you won't receive a call from them again. It is painful to understand, but it is the absolute truth.

I went through it, firsthand. The physical stuff is *gone forever*. But peace came when I understood Blaise's beingness had transformed, like the caterpillar hanging upside down within a chrysalis, radically transforming into something crazy beautiful, and finally emerging as a colorful butterfly. However, the transformation of a loved one from life to death is much more dramatic and powerful. I believe your *only* way to freedom and your return to sanity here in this world is to tap into meditation. With this practice, you will understand what evolution from the physical to the spiritual truly means.

The Importance of Meditation as We Go through Grief

The knowledge will dawn on you, powerfully, like nothing else in your life—*they have never and will never leave you.* Your child's death is *not meant* to make any sense, at least in terms of what our naked eye sees and our other four senses perceive. Let go of the "why." Since there is no magic pill or quick fix to cure the grief inside, the solution, therefore, lies in our connection with the spiritual world, which is accessible to everyone 24/7. It's where we can find our children's guidance during this most difficult time. This is where we access our inner wisdom, through a meditation practice that bridges the physical to the spiritual and to the sacred world of the intuition *we all possess.* And when we do, we will find that it teaches us that *their life still continues* because it has *transformed.*

Dr. Deepak Chopra's suggestions on quieting the mind until you get to its source, which is pure consciousness, saved my life. I realized that my initial overwhelming, relentlessly painful thoughts were only that—thoughts. As he teaches, we aren't our thoughts; we are the consciousness in which they flow in and out. Consciousness is ever present and still. And as we observe those thoughts coming and going, we let our being at the core of it all be the spectator. We are always safe, because we are the audience.

Every single thing in nature transforms, but that doesn't mean that we are disconnected from what has transformed! It's completely up to us to bridge that gap. This intuitive bridge connects Blaise and me in a different way, and that's the game changer. He never left at all. We have to *intuitively connect with our children from now on.* I do it every single day during my early morning and evening meditation practice. It is such an amazing experience of love and beauty and light!

I feel his beingness and his peace, because when I tap into a world of joy and sacredness, I feel the Oneness between him and everything else. I am definitely a part of that Oneness—pure joy and love. This bond makes me feel light and energized. Every single thing in nature transforms, and as humans, we obviously aren't excluded from the equation. We just have to be willing to tap into our natural, sacred intuition. Intuition is the key to many, many of our "human" questions.

"The intuitive mind is a sacred gift and the rational mind is a faithful servant. We have created a society that honors the servant and has forgotten the gift."
Albert Einstein

What if Death Is Just the Beginning of Life?

This book also explores why it's important to overcome difficulties no matter what, by creating something beautiful in the wake of whatever has befallen you—death, divorce, disease, destruction from natural and man-made disasters, or other upheavals. The terrible times you suffer are not the end of life but can become a new beginning.

As a nonprofit photographer and philanthropist who has worked all over the world, I can attest that everywhere I go, I encounter ordinary people who've accomplished extraordinary things. Profiles in courage, towering love, and passion, people's transformational stories all have one thing in common: they have risen out of their own pain by lifting up others. These everyday heroes have much to show us about how to live life wholeheartedly. **If they can do it, so can we.**

Many of the people I have met, thanks to my travels and work, have overcome tremendous odds and converted their personal suffering into empathy for those going through the same challenges, and have helped the world become a safer, kinder place. In my experience, if we focus our attention on the lessons that are oftentimes hidden within life's challenges, the pain itself can be a catalyst for positive change. I believe I have a human responsibility to lift up as many people as possible with the fables and poems in this book. It is my hope that these stories will act as a balm for those going through their grief and dark moments. It is also my intention to create a physical healing center with twenty-one deep, holistic modalities that will be my pragmatic way of offering my wholehearted understanding and compassion to those who need it.

This journey of grieving has taught me that nothing lasts forever except our relationship with the universe. We don't have to be who we were yesterday. If we understand that everything in life is impermanent, we can accept not having tomorrow what we have today, and also of having tomorrow what we *don't* have today. Because of the exciting opportunity every challenge creates, we have the choice to love and choose joy instead of despair. It is also my experience that this healing form of self-love can save lives—**where there is love, there is life**.

The experience of writing this book turned out to be an enormous learning curve. In the process, I discovered a great deal more about myself, what I am capable of if I focus my energy on positive thinking, and why it is so important to look at things from a higher perspective. In an attempt to let out my unbearable pain in a cathartic way, I unearthed my infinite inner strength, wisdom, and a unique ability to move forward in a positive way, because I know it's exactly what Blaise would have wanted.

My journey through my initial uncontrollable pain, all the setbacks I experienced while trying to bridge the physical with the spiritual, and the slow process of healing, which continues to this day, are all portrayed in this book. The following twenty-one fables are part of that healing process, and they showcase how to keep your glow alive, that beautiful spirit of yours, amid all the uncertainty and confusion. They unveil twenty-one pieces of wisdom that celebrate life in all its forms and will help you transform your pain into healing. I'm honored to be a part of your transformative journey.

THE WEAVER

By Grant Colfax Tullar

My life is but a weaving
Between my God and me.
I cannot choose the color
He weaveth steadily.
Oft' times He weaveth sorrow;
And I in foolish pride
Forget He sees the upper
And I the underside.
Not 'til the loom is silent
And the shuttles cease to fly
Will God unroll the canvas
And reveal the reason why.
The dark threads are as needful
In the weaver's skillful hand
As the threads of gold and silver
In the pattern He has planned.
He knows, He loves, He cares;
Nothing this truth can dim.
He gives the very best to those
Who leave the choice to Him.

I have always really loved this poem by Grant Colfax Tullar. It speaks of God, the creative force behind everything, and the way He weaves our lives in the same way a tapestry is woven.

How appropriate, when I think of you and me. How appropriate, when I know that every day you infuse me with beautiful, positive ideas, and with the courage to keep going, even stronger than before! How appropriate, when I never knew that we would be separated so early in the flesh, but united more than ever in spirit! How appropriate, when we just can't control the outcome of anything. How appropriate, when we learn to go with what the universe has envisioned for us all along.

CAMEL
AND SPIDER

nce upon a time, Camel and Spider became friends as they crossed a great desert. Spider wasn't like the regular household spiders that annoy and scare you, or the small ones that take shelter in your bathtub and spin webs in the hardest-to-reach corners of your house.

No, this spider was very, very different. You might shriek five times louder at the mere sight of Spider, because this spider was a tarantula. And that meant she was bigger and hairier than any spider you've ever seen in your life! She was as big as your face . . . but her personality was as sweet as honey.

But to Camel, Spider seemed tiny.

If you know anything about crossing deserts, you know it can be a very lonely experience. When Camel and Spider met each other, even though one was very tall (although small in stature for most camels) and the other very small (although very big compared to most spiders), they became fast friends. And good friends are hard to find.

Camel slowed down to match Spider's pace, and Spider quickened hers to keep up with Camel. They were on a very important mission: They needed to get to the watering hole.

If you know anything about deserts, you know water is very scarce and watering holes are very important. Animals have instincts for things that you and I don't. It's in their blood to be able to sniff out water and find it. But the oasis was still very, very far away.

"I don't think we'll ever find the water hole," Camel said.

"Why?" Spider sweetly asked.

Camel said, "Well, we've been traveling for days and days and days and days and days and days . . ."

Spider joined in. "And days and days and days and days and days . . . but . . . we can see the sun and have sought great shelters at night. We've been so very lucky."

Camel snorted and then spit. Not because he was annoyed at all. It's just what camels do. Camels are actually quite patient, kind, and most of all, they are very, very smart.

"You found the shelter, not me," Camel said. He said this because he didn't like it very much when Spider disappeared at night. He missed Spider when she did what spiders do in the desert . . . burrow underground. He also was very afraid of the dark.

Spider caused Camel a great amount of stress and worry during their nights together. Every night, he wondered if Spider would come out of her hole in the morning. So, Camel treated every day of their friendship as if it were their last. This meant he was always on his best behavior, and Spider was always dear to Camel.

Camels don't burrow into holes in the sand. They are too big. Instead, they lay in the sand. Camel loved laying in the light of the full moon most of all. And that night, the moon was the fullest it had ever been because the moon was very close to the Earth.

"Good night, Camel," Spider said.

"Good night, Spider," Camel said.

Spider burrowed into the sand and disappeared.

All that night, Camel worried. He sat there in the light of the moon and watched the sand dunes, calm and beautiful, ripple like waves on an ocean of land. He would never see the dunes with Spider at night. He sighed. Somehow, the beauty of the desert didn't seem real unless he shared it with Spider. Still, the moon was round like Spider, and so he talked to the moon all night as if Spider was right beside him.

Finally, the sun rose.

"Good morning, Camel!" Spider said.

"Good morning, Spider!" Camel said.

His heart felt as full as the moon when she dug herself out of her burrow.

They set back out on their way across the desert. Spider's eight hairy nimble legs moved oh so quickly compared to Camel's huge hooves.

"I think we're almost there!" Spider said.

"You always say that," Camel said.

"Well, we get a little closer every day," Spider said.

Then a terrible wind stirred up the desert. The storm lasted for days and days and days, and the wind blew Spider away. Far, far away.

Camel went in search of Spider in the harsh wind, but his eyes got pelted with little grains of sand, and so all he could do was wait until it was over.

He waited and waited and waited and waited. He hated waiting and waiting and waiting.

When all finally felt calm, Camel yelled, "Spider? Spider? Where are you?"

Spider didn't answer. She was very, very far away . . . no telling where.

Camel went all over the desert trying to find her. He hoped he would come upon her like he did the very first time they met, as she scurried up a sand dune and then slipped back down the sand. She loved to play.

The nights were long. But at least he had the moon to keep him company. He talked to Spider through the moon and told her about his day.

"I miss you," Camel said, longing for his friend.

Finally, Camel set off for the watering hole again. Camels, unlike Spiders, can go for great distances in the desert without needing water. But even Camel had grown desperately thirsty.

It took five more days for Camel to reach the watering hole. As he sat by the banks of the watering hole, surrounded by palm trees, he felt so happy and sad at the same time. Spider and Camel had talked about this moment for a very long time. But at this moment, Camel felt like only half a Camel. Spider helped him feel whole. So, he only felt a deep sadness instead of what should have been great pleasure as he licked up the fresh water.

He drank and drank and drank and got so tired he took a nap.

When he woke up, Spider had crawled on his nose to take a nap. Naeltim, the sylph of the air, had made sure that Spider's journey landed her safely in the oasis.

"Spider! You're here!"

"What took you so long?" Spider said. "I've been waiting for you."

"I looked everywhere for you!"

"Too bad camels can't fly!" Spider said. "The wind blew me here so very far, so very fast. All I had to do was relax. I missed you. You've taken a very long time to get here."

"I didn't walk as fast without you," said Camel.

"Silly Camel, I'm right here with you even when I'm not with you."

Camel looked at the moon, visible in the afternoon sky. "You're in the moon. You're in every grain of sand. I can't see anything without seeing you, Spider."

SPIRIT

ONE THING

One thing that makes me so pissed off,
is you leaving me like this.
How could you do that
You got consumed
And burned yourself to death
For no reason
When you truly had it all
I can't say that I did not try my very best with
you
And my very best is the best of the best
I go to the edges of the world to accomplish
what I want to accomplish
And you know that
I am so hurt
I am so hurt
Because my Love for you was the best
And it still is
But you are no longer there to listen
And no longer there to take from me
With a smirk you left me
In this motionless reality
That makes no sense

Without you talking to me
Without you driving me crazy
And without you making me comfortable with
my choices
The smell of gunpowder permeates my
nostrils
And screams words of helplessness
Although I shake my head, clearly knowing
that you are
You are here, molded into the everything
And into this perfect nothingness

September 14, 2019
Bloomfield, Connecticut

THE BOY
AND THE
BRONZE STATUE

hen the boy turned fourteen years old, he ran away from his family because he didn't feel understood by anyone, not even those closest to him. The people who were supposed to love him to the moon and back didn't see him at all. Everyone made fun of him because of his gentle heart, and he couldn't understand the injustice, prejudice, and ill-manners among his family members. There seemed to always be misunderstandings and altercations, screaming and harshness.

His family was very wealthy and only loved money. The thing they wanted most in life was to make more money and watch the gold pile up so high in their safes that they would have to order bigger, better, and more secure safes to store all their wealth. Other people were of no consequence, unless they could lead the family to more successful deals, which led to more bars of gold. The only people they were friendly to were their security guards, the ones in charge of watching their money, gold, and stock certificates twenty-four hours a day, seven days a week. The boy's family of users and loan sharks didn't care for the feelings of others unless it could profit them in a big way.

Because the family had so much money, they made their home completely dark. They felt they could better see the burglars' flashlights and be alerted to break-ins that way. After all, burglars can't burgle in the dark now, can they? The family's fear of being robbed led to paranoia. Outsiders were never to be trusted, not that anyone in the family trusted each other at all either. But strangers—especially altruistic people with great intentions and ideas that might help the world— were definitely not welcome, and particularly not if these people ever asked them to part with any wealth to help a noble cause. Nothing made the boy's family sicker to their stomachs than being asked for donations.

And it's a good thing that strangers weren't welcome, for if they were, they would have found the deepest, darkest, most depressing mansion. Sure, it was grand, and sure the family filled it with precious artifacts, paintings, and sculptures. But whenever the sun shone, Sebastien the butler drew massive, dark red velvet drapes over the windows to keep the sun out. The sun was "damaging to the priceless works."

One day, the boy grew tired of living in the darkness, and he slipped out of the house to go on a hike in the woods. The beautiful colors of spring inspired him so much that when he got home, he pulled back the curtains and spent the entire afternoon painting in the glorious sunlight, filling a canvas with what he'd seen. He left it on the easel and fell asleep on one of the leather sofas while admiring his work.

When his mother found him asleep, she yelled at him.

"What on earth do you think you're doing?! Sebastien! Close the curtains IMMEDIATELY!"

The boy awoke, completely confused by what was going on. Where was he? His dream had been filled with the most brilliant colors and had made him feel so peaceful and content. Just before his mother had entered the room, with her heels clacking on the parquet floor, he had been dreaming of taking a stroll with a butterfly that swooped in and out along the path where he walked. Every few seconds the butterfly had landed to check him out, to notice him.

Right before his mother had awakened the boy, the butterfly had said, "Wake up! Don't be afraid. I will always fly with you."

Sebastien closed the velvet curtains, and the room fell into darkness. The boy remembered what the butterfly had said, but it was hard to be brave. It was harder to be himself in a dreary house where his family didn't know him. It was impossible to remember that the butterfly was still at his side.

The boy's mother pointed to his painting. "Out with this TRASH!"

Sebastien looked as if she'd just punched him in the gut. Sebastien knew that the boy loved to paint, and how can one paint in the dark?

Sebastien picked up the painting. "I will dispose of this painting, Madame," Sebastien said, and carried it out of the room.

The boy broke down in tears.

"Stop being so sensitive! If you can't act like a man and toughen up, we will send you to boarding school! They'll teach you about discipline there. They'll make you strong," his mother said.

After that incident, no one in the family spoke to him very much. The boy learned how to stay silent because there weren't any meaningful conversations, only conversations about how to get MORE and MORE money. It was an addiction of the coldest kind.

The boy wanted to help the world by ending his family's exploitation of others, their greediness, and their lack of compassion. And so he decided to teach them a lesson, to help them see the true meaning of life. He wanted to somehow bring his family out of their selfish, greedy ways and into larger worlds through the light of service to others and a joy that they'd never known: love.

The boy used his artistic skills in secret, so he became an apprentice at a local sculptor's studio. There, he learned how to turn clay into great masterpieces. He had a natural ability in the arts, and while he loved painting, the three-dimensional world held a special fascination for him. He imagined that, as he sculpted the clay, he recreated himself and freed himself of the terrible obligation to be silent whenever he was around them. With each sculpture he completed, the clay statues became more like real people, and sometimes he spoke with them.

"I don't understand, my family is very rich, but the money is never enough," he said to his most recent creation, a boy with a javelin in his hand, frozen at the moment just before hurling it into space.

The boy looked into the javelin thrower's eyes and said, "They want more and more power, and to be the richest family of all, but I only see value in art . . . in you." What the boy enjoyed most of all was how his creations listened.

He also loved the view of Prague from the studio windows. It was dusk, and the sun was setting over the Vltava River. At this time of the evening, when the angle of the sun was just right, Prague turned into something out of a fairytale. Orange and yellow, tangerine and purple, the sunlight floated along the water as if to say, *Come away with me, to another land, another place inside your heart.* From where he stood, with his hands stiff and dirty from working the clay, the boy could see and hear the chimes of the Prague Astronomical Clock, the oldest of its kind in the world.

As the last chime sounded, a harp's music floated magically through the air. Different subtle notes played, running after each other. A misty rain fell, and the small droplets mixed with the twinkling lights of the buildings in the distance to create pure magic. The boy's heart lightened as he started to run, and the noises around him became muffled. Every other sound faded away except his own heavy breathing. The river Vltava ran quietly alongside the walkway as the boy ran up to the top of the hill that overlooked the magical city, and for the first time he noticed an enchanting castle.

He walked toward the castle, crouched over, and sat in a corner of the empty square, in the shadow of a few bronze statues. He didn't pay attention to anything else but his own thoughts and sadness. He suddenly felt lost and lonely as his thoughts turned back toward the difficulties he had with his family. Only his artwork understood him. The world felt harsh, and it was getting harder and harder to imagine the butterfly from his dream was always with him. He longed to free the world of his family's exploitation, but how?

Suddenly, one of the bronze statues in the square spoke to the boy.

"Why are you sad, Boy?" said the statue of a man on a horse. As soon as the statue spoke, one of the last rays of sun graced the face of the statue. His soft, gentle voice startled the boy because he wasn't used to being spoken to, least of all by talking bronze statues.

"Who are you?" the boy asked, trembling.

"I was once a man, living and breathing, like you," the statue said.

The boy trembled even more.

"I memorialize a man who once lived, and now we are both eternal. Remember that whatever you do here on Earth is eternal. What you do matters. If you're driven to money, that money will dissipate eventually. If you spread love and fight against sorrow and heartache, your deeds will echo forever among future generations. That is why the family of the man I represent created me. Your family will not have a statue made for them, because as soon as their money dissipates, or as soon as someone more powerful subjugates them, they will no longer be remembered."

"What are you remembered for, Statue?" the boy asked.

"They say that I am remembered for my bravery, Boy. I slayed a dragon and that is how I am now remembered."

"I'm not brave, Statue. I don't even know what brave means!"

"I also wasn't brave. I used to be a shy, sensitive boy just like yourself until I realized that I could use my vulnerability to help the vulnerable. You see, in Latin, the ancient language I spoke, *vulnera* means *wounds*. Because I had been wounded myself, I knew what it felt like, and I decided to help heal the wounds of others. I became a warrior, and I slayed a dragon!"

"You killed a real dragon?"

"Yes! I am known for killing a dragon on the flat-topped Dragon Hill and it is said that no grass ever grows where the dragon's blood trickled down!"

"Is that why you have become a statue? Because you became a warrior, and you killed a dragon?" the boy asked.

"A statue is what people make to remember people's deeds. I am not the statue; the statue just reminds people of my life and my deeds."

"If you are not the statue, who are you?"

"I am what I make you feel. If they didn't make a statue, it would be very difficult for people to remember what I did. People love statues and what they represent. Statues represent the outside of people. It is necessary to make the statues because people's physical forms don't last. Our deeds define us because they spring from our innermost desires and our most precious possession of all—our hearts. Bravery creates great deeds that last forever. Even if it is only to speak one's mind."

"I don't know anyone who has done good deeds like you, Statue. My family only believes in taking advantage of others. They are greedy and hurtful. I don't know any better," the boy said.

"Boy, the world is full of good people who do good deeds. Their deeds are just typically not as noticed as the bad ones. People love drama and power and money and the excitement that comes from conflict. It is much easier to want to make money for yourself and accumulate power than it is to give it all up and focus on giving money to those who don't have it or fighting for a just cause."

"How did you do it, Statue, if you were vulnerable?"

"I had a rare ability to feel the sensitivity and emotions of others, just like they were my own. To overcome my sensitivity, I first had to accept myself. I couldn't become what others wanted me to be. Instead of letting my emotions act like a runaway horse, I pulled on their reins and then released them when the time was right. I responded instead of reacting. And guess what? That's also how I learned to ride my horse, Uffington! We became inseparable."

"So, you learned to help the world by riding Uffington?"

"In a way. I learned how to help the world by riding Uffington and by riding the waves of my emotions. Because I could feel the emotions of others, I learned to tune into them without owning them. I learned the strength of knowing what mattered to me, my values, and not having other people's emotions and opinions thrust upon me. I had to learn what parts of life were mine and what parts were not. Thanks to Uffington, I learned to be strong and to live a balanced life."

"How beautiful, Statue. I want to help people remember the good deeds of other people. I want to learn how to make statues like yourself, so that people remember other people's good deeds. I want to become a craftsman who helps others."

"Boy, you have found yourself and you have a noble heart. Therefore, you are no longer lost, and are very brave, indeed. Find your own balance and pace just like I did. This will allow you to reserve all your energy to help others and make a tremendous impact on the world. You have an eye for beauty and art. You can and WILL make a big difference in this world, because the world needs beautiful and sensitive people like yourself. The world needs people like you, so that they can see what only you can see. Be true to who you are."

Just then, a familiar-looking butterfly swooped down on the breath of Naeltim, the sylph of the air. The winged creature flew all around the boy, just as it had in his dream. The boy's gaze followed the butterfly flitting from bush to bush, and a sense of peace filled him from the inside out. Being all alone in the world with only the butterfly for a companion would be better than becoming someone his family wanted him to be.

"Thank you, Statue, I'll try. By the way, what's your name?"

"They call me Saint George. But, remember, Boy, it is not my name that matters. Slaying the dragon is what made all the difference in the world."

STRENGTH IN SENSITIVITY

ONE LOVE

One thing that I can tell you is, my Love for
you is the same
And what I can say to you is that
you are keeping me ablaze
In your name I want to continue
In the name of you and in the name of Love
I want to continue
I know it was too difficult to be here
And I am probably the only one who gets it
I know what you and I went through
And I know how sensitive you were
Your beautiful sensitivity was attacked
But I will now protect it forever
And create the most beautiful sacred spaces
All in your honor
And in honor of the efforts that
took for you to be here,
You beautiful soul.
Your name will be all over the place
Reminding people of what Love is
And that Love does not die
Because it is, in fact, the one and only
That lives on Forever.

September 15, 2019
Bloomfield, Connecticut

THE WALTZ
OF THE
HONEYBEES

 nce upon a time, there was a wonderful beehive filled with majestic honeybees nestled within a sprawling orchard in picturesque Velvety Oak. Deep within this hive lived a bee named Wanda, who didn't love flying at all. What she did love was letting her little legs skate across the honeycomb as she waltzed to the buzzing sound of the honeybees. She was exhausted from making honey all summer, and long into the fall. All she wanted to do was dance and rest her weary wings.

While she whiled away the hours waltzing, her fellow honeybees busily made as much honey as they could before wintertime. As winter was fast approaching, there was no time for anything else but fly from the hive to harvest, pollen off of the fragrant flowers nearby, and then busily store it within the thousands of honeycombs in the hive. Many bees took their turn, hundreds of times over, to help each other store the pollen and create golden honey from the flowers' sweet nectar that would become the bees' lifeline during the coming snowstorms.

But all Wanda wanted to do was dance around the honeycomb.

Every year, the majestic bees built their huge honeycomb in the shape of a heart, and once the heart-shaped honeycomb was completed, wintertime arrived. Winter was the season that Wanda loved the most because she could waltz all she wanted while the other bees slept and slept and slept, their bellies full of life-giving honey and their wings tired from their buzzing.

The honeycomb had become something of a wonder in Velvety Oak, a wonder that the humans enjoyed all winter long.

Each year, the bees heard shouts of, "Oh my goodness look, the heart is here!"

"Look, it's back, it's back!"

"Winter must be coming! No more summer sun. No more swimming in the river."

"Soon we'll have a winter wonderland of snow to play in!"

For some, the sight of the heart caused extreme joy; for others, it caused a touch of sorrow; and for yet another, a small gnome Velvety Oak—who was up to no good—it caused another feeling entirely. But for the honeybees, the construction of the honeycomb heart meant the completion of all their hard work and the comfort of knowing that they would be able to enjoy the fruits of their labor—a refuge in the winter storms and enough honey to last them until next spring.

Each year on the winter solstice, the honeybees coated the last part of the honeycomb with wax, and then their heart-shaped honeycomb was complete. Only then did the first snowflake fall on Velvety Oak. And Wanda always let out a huge sigh of relief on that day, because she could finally begin to waltz the winter away. What joy she had on that day!

When the first snowflake fell, everyone in Velvety Oak put all their honey away for the long, long winter. Each time they pulled it out and tasted it, they remembered the long, hard labors of the majestic bees that whirled away the summer days making their special treat. And they remembered how everyone in Velvety Oak worked together in harmony all summer and into the fall to finish the great harvest and store its bounty for the cold months ahead. And they remembered the cold, heart-shaped honeycomb that sat out in the snow, protecting the honeybees from the wicked winter chill.

On the night of the winter solstice, the entire town gathered together around their fireplaces to drink a special warm honey drink and toast the health of the honeybees to thank them for the special nectar that would get them through the treacherous winter.

But one particular year, when the winter solstice was its fiercest and the honey was at its sweetest, while everyone else toasted the majestic honeybees, one lonely gnome crossed the tundra of the frozen orchard. The traveling gnome came upon the heart-shaped honeycomb, and because he was starving and so very cold, he took a bite out of it. The honey enchanted his taste buds and warmed him all the way down to his large potbelly. He was so hungry from his travels and felt faint and light-headed.

But in a heartbeat, winter changed into summer once again.

The honeybees woke up to Wanda waltzing in her honeycomb. They had tears in their eyes. Wanda stopped waltzing. The thick floor of the honeycomb had warmed in the summer sun, becoming sticky and gooey, trapping her feet into stillness.

"Whatever is the matter?" Wanda said at the sight of so many frightened honeybees.

"Look and see!" one of her honeybee friends said. Together, they all flew to the gaping hole in the once beautiful honeycomb.

"What's happened?" Wanda asked.

"We don't know!" a group of her honeybee friends exclaimed.

Wanda flew out of the hole to investigate. She had no idea why the air wasn't cold anymore and the grass was green again. Confused, she fluttered to the meadow and saw flowers blooming.

"No! This can't beeeeeeeeeeeee!" Wanda said, buzzing around.

But it was.

"I'll never get to waltz now! We'll have to get back to work again!"

She fluttered and fluttered, trying to return to the hive, to her honeybee family, with her heavy, sticky bee feet trailing behind her in the wind. During her flight home, she spotted someone asleep in the heather. He was a strange creature that Wanda had never seen before, with small little ears and a big pot belly, and smiling from ear to ear with honey smeared all around his mouth.

"Do you know what you've done?" Wanda said as she buzzed around his big bulbous nose.

He didn't move very much and only tried to sleepily swat her away.

"How dare you! Get up, little man! Get up!" Wanda said.

But he slept and slept and slept, his belly full of golden honey.

As she buzzed around trying to wake the gnome, her honeybee family buzzed by in a hurry, busily harvesting nectar and bringing it back to the hive. It was like watching a bee parade. They were determined and kept their wings fluttering non-stop!

"No, no, no, no! That's not what we should be doing!" she yelled at her honeybee family. "You should be asleep, and I should be dancing . . ." Wanda was not happy at all about the sun shining brightly on her wings or her sticky dancing feet.

But her honeybee family didn't mind the bother at all. They all had faces as sunshiny as the gorgeous day, more determined than ever to forget that they didn't have a whole winter off from their labor. But they didn't see it like that at all. See, they loved their work, and when you love your work, it isn't work at all!

Wanda didn't understand.

She dutifully went to the field of heather and soaked up the nectar, then flew back to the hive with her honeybee brothers and sisters. Eventually, after a few days, the heart was again complete, the snow fell again, and the villagers sat by their cozy fires knowing that the bees were safe in their heart-shaped honeycomb home.

But there in the field of heather, the snowflakes woke the gnome from his slumber. He stood up in the field of purple flowers and took a big whiff of the air. He held his huge belly with his tiny hands and waddled down the snow-covered path all the way back to where the repaired heart-shaped honeycomb hung from the oak tree, shuddering in the winter wind.

Inside, Wanda was waltzing away happily. She'd forgotten all about the interruption to her waltz, and instead had lost herself completely in the buzzing of her slumbering honeybee family and the music her fluttering heart made, keeping the perfect beat for her dance.

But then the hive shook so hard that Wanda slammed through a comb and took a bath in honey. She tried and tried to get herself free from the tasty goop, but she couldn't free herself. As she flailed her little legs and wings to get out of the honey, she sunk deeper and deeper.

"Heeelp!" Wanda's little honey voice cried.

Just as the gnome was chewing up one of the parts of the honeycomb, he heard Wanda's cry for help. He realized she was in the palm of his hand, trying to swim and sinking in the part of the honeycomb that he was about to eat.

Wanda's tears filled the comb.

"Whatever is the matter?" the gnome said as the sun began to shine and melt away the snow again.

"I'll never waltz again!"

"What's a waltz?

This just made Wanda more upset, and she couldn't answer. She was about to sink all the way down into the honeycomb in the palm of the gnome's hand. The gnome picked a blade of grass for her to catch hold of and helped her climb out of the comb and into his other hand. It took her awhile to catch her breath. She coughed up honey for quite some time.

Just then, a large swarm of honeybees emerged from the damaged, heart-shaped honeycomb, and they flew back to the heather fields. There were hundreds of them.

"Where are they going?" the gnome said.

"They're going to do what they always do. They're sipping nectar to make honey and build their heart-shaped home."

"Home?"

"Yes."

"You mean you all live together?"

"Yes."

The gnome sighed.

"Where's your home?" Wanda asked

"I live in a solitary cavern in the woods. And I got lonely," he said.

"And hungry," Wanda added.

"Gnomes are always hungry," he said, holding his very big belly with one hand. "I didn't know I ate your home."

"Don't worry, my friends and sisters and I will fix it again," Wanda said.

"I do apologize. You see, I've never seen or tasted anything like your home and this . . . honey, you call it?"

Wanda nodded, her eyes wide.

"How incredible and exciting to have a family so large! You must have so much fun together. I've never seen anything that bustling! Honey tastes so much better than the mushrooms I normally eat."

"Well, do you want to know the truth?" Wanda asked.

"I like it when everyone is asleep," Wanda said.

"Why?" the gnome asked, his eyes wide too.

"Then I can waltz all by myself. See, I love building the house with my family. But I love waltzing all alone even more."

The gnome carried Wanda to a little pond not far from the torn, heart-shaped honeycomb. He placed her on the edge of the grass and Wanda soaked her little body in the pond, fluttered her wings, and basked in the sunshine to get un-sticky. The gnome liked watching her tend to her delicate wings.

Together they watched the parade of her honeybee brothers and sisters repairing the hive.

"Thanks for not being angry," the gnome said. "I wish I could be a honeybee."

"Whatever for?" Wanda asked, fluttering her wings in the breeze to dry them off.

"So I could build a beautiful home with a family and have some company," he said.

"Well, you could always come to visit me next spring. After I'm done waltzing," Wanda said with a smile.

The gnome smiled back.

"I better hurry back. I don't want to get locked out of the hive; they're nearly finished!" Wanda said. "See you in the spring?"

"Yes, see you then!" the gnome said, giving her a lift up to the nearly completed honeycomb.

The gnome watched as Wanda, a grin spread across her face , disappeared inside. The last of the honeybees buzzed back to the hive, and they smoothed over the heart-shaped comb one more time. As it hung from the branch of the old oak tree, Naeltim, the sylph of the air, blew his cold, icy wind. The first snowflake fell onto the gnome's bulbous nose. A flurry of snow soon followed the first flake.

Then the gnome waltzed up the path to gnomeland, where he ate some mushrooms he'd foraged from the forest and dreamed of seeing Wanda again next spring.

COOPERATION

BECAUSE YOU ARE NOT MY SON

Because you are not my son
Ours is a fable
Woven into a celestial garden
And I am Fire
As the dance continues,
I am there to ignite
And remind you that I am Fire
And won't let go
Because you are not my son
You are the celestial garden
Dancing while I ignite
Forever
In the Love that we all are.

October 29, 2019
Boulder, Colorado

THE ENCHANTMENT
OF THE KINGDOM
OF EMERALDS
AND RUBIES

ne enchanted evening, along the shores of the sparkliest and coolest stream in the only undiscovered place in the world, Queen Corraelis sat at her window at the very tippy-top of the very tallest spire of her castle. She looked out upon the Kingdom of Emeralds and Rubies, where she had ruled all her life, and which was the most charming and delightful kingdom in all of history and where everything shone brightly and reflected all the colors of the rainbow.

All the queen's subjects were very happy and got along perfectly with one another because there was no shortage of anything. Actually, there was so much abundance that everyone owned beautiful houses made entirely of emeralds and rubies. Even their beds, dining tables, and toothbrushes were fashioned out of emeralds and rubies.

Because her subjects lacked for nothing, friendships reigned perfectly among the kingdom's inhabitants. They knew nothing about greed or jealousy. They only desired to be themselves and didn't think much about other people's journeys or thoughts. Because everything was perfect and shiny and colorful and the sun shone every day, there was no rain in the Kingdom of Emeralds and Rubies, but the colorful plants and flowers thrived anyway because love made everything grow abundantly.

Besides the most beautiful and compassionate Queen Corraelis, many other gorgeous and whimsical creatures lived in the kingdom. Colorful woodpeckers, red squirrels, vermilion birds, ebony martins, and leather-toned owls lived among the trees. Happy cows grazed in the company of a bevy of azure dragons and rainbow serpents, who spent their time sunbathing in the pastures or playing in the sparkling sunshine overhead, creating an awe-inspiring vision. The spectacle even stopped carriage traffic, especially at night when the moon was full and the sparkles were the sparkliest.

The kingdom ran perfectly because the queen had given everyone particular duties to perform. Cheerful gnomes helped build each other's homes and cultivated their gardens. Golden elves had the distinct honor of helping to build bridges and roads for the giants of the kingdom. The giants helped with positioning the emeralds and rubies on the roofs of the gnomes' and elves' houses, leaving the elves to help place the gems on the teeny-tiny homes of the river fairies.

As beautiful blue butterflies flew around singing lovely melodies, flowers sprung open in all their glory, and the bumblebees caressed the flowers' petals as the bees buzzed by to gather nectar at the ever-blooming rose garden that grew on the banks of the sparkly stream.

Each enchanted evening, everyone gathered together by the sparkly stream to celebrate life and love. They all sang happy and melodious songs that made the rainbow lorikeets and the bluebirds of paradise dance in the sky in celebration of another sensational day of togetherness. Since the beginning of her reign, which dated back to the beginning of time, Queen Corraelis had never missed an evening celebration. The queen possessed a beautiful singing phoenix that kept her immortal. She had it guarded closely day and night by a fire-breathing dragon in one of the corners of her great royal bedroom chamber. The phoenix always sang the sweetest when love was true.

Everything was happy and perfectly harmonious, until the day after the sixteenth birthday of Princess Eiliope, the daughter of Queen Corraelis and the dead king, who had died when the princess was just a baby. He had been wounded during a battle with a neighboring kingdom that had threatened to overrun the Kingdom of Emeralds and Rubies. The princess missed her dad terribly, and her sadness caused a deep hole in the middle of her heart that could never be filled.

Her resentment led her to become more and more greedy. Over time, she wanted more emeralds and more rubies than anyone else in the kingdom. She was the princess, after all. She said she needed them to create a sparkly stream of emeralds and rubies in her room.

The queen, who had unlimited resources of emeralds and rubies, kept granting the princess more and more gems, because there was no shortage of precious stones in the Kingdom of Emeralds and Rubies. The queen saw no harm in giving more and more precious stones to those who asked because her love for her people was boundless. When Queen Corraelis granted Princess Eiliope all the gems, she felt a sense of joy for having met all of the princess's needs. Nothing made the queen happier or more sparkly.

But something not so shiny or sparkly had entered the kingdom the day Princess Eiliope made her first request for more gems. You see, the princess decided to use the queen's compassion to her advantage and concocted a scheme to get what she always wanted. The princess realized that she could ask for more of whatever she wished because the queen had never said no. Not one time.

And this emboldened Princess Eiliope to think more unshiny and more unsparkly thoughts. Finally, one day, Princess Eiliope decided that she wanted to be queen herself. She was tired of being a princess. So, she went to the queen and played a trick on her. She told her the truth as if it was a lie.

"Why can't I be queen and have my own throne with emeralds and rubies? My own scepter with emeralds and rubies? Why do I have to have my house, my dinner table and chairs and bed, and even my toothbrush made from emeralds and rubies, like everyone else? I don't want to be like everyone else. I want to have what the queen has. I want the singing phoenix so I can live forever too!" Eiliope exclaimed to Queen Corraelis.

The queen was very surprised when Princess Eiliope made her request. "Why? I have granted you everything that you have ever requested, every time, because there is no shortage of anything here in the Kingdom of Emeralds and Rubies. Isn't that enough?"

"No! You don't do more for me than you do for your lowly servants. I don't want to be like everyone else! I want to be special!" the princess said, stomping her feet.

Queen Corraelis, a very compassionate and sensitive queen, became very sad. She couldn't understand why Eiliope wasn't happy with her abundant life and all of the emeralds and rubies in it. She thought carefully and said, "Darling, you must learn to find happiness not in emeralds or in rubies or in being more advantaged than other people. You must find your treasure in things not of this world."

Eiliope took one last look at the caged, golden phoenix sitting on a perch behind the huge fire-breathing dragon in her mother's chambers.

"That's easy to say when you will live forever, with all the emeralds and rubies you desire, always beautiful and never aging. But I will age. I will grow old. It's not fair. I want to be beautiful forever, like you!" She turned on her heel and left the room.

Now, Princess Eiliope hadn't inherited her mother's immortality, but she had inherited her father's magic cloak. She had used it to play tricks on people ever since she learned how to wield its power. She decided to call a guard into her room. And when he entered, she ordered him to sit down.

When he did, the princess placed her magic cloak over the man's head and whispered an incantation.

In an instant, he turned into a handsome king, dressed in a cape spun of gold with emeralds and rubies dotting the fabric. The green and red gems glistened in the candlelight of the princess's room.

"You will go to my mother and profess your love for her. You will kiss her hand. The moment you kiss her hand she will not be able to refuse you anything. You will ask her to marry you," the princess said with a smile.

The one-time guard's glassy eyes brightened. It was as if he'd been breathing life into the body he now possessed and believed every word of the enchantment. His confidence grew with every step he took down the long royal corridors toward the queen's chambers. And before long he knocked on the queen's door. When the castle guards allowed him entry into the chamber, the phoenix stopped singing sweetly and instead sang loudly.

"May I have your hand, my beautiful Queen?"

Queen Corraelis hesitated, watching her favorite bird. She listened to the phoenix's song as if in a trance. Slowly, she raised her hand to meet his. He clasped her hand and kissed it immediately. "Will you marry me?" he said.

The phoenix screeched.

Queen Corraelis said, "I will."

"I promise you to give you all the pearls and diamonds of my kingdom, and the sapphires too. But you have to abdicate your throne if you want to marry me."

"Of course," the queen said.

The next day, there was a grand wedding celebration. The phoenix was in a state, no longer singing but screeching. No one could figure out why or how to calm it down. No earthly creature knew that the king was a fake and that the queen was about to forfeit her kingdom and her immortality. Eiliope even helped her mother prepare for her special day by handing her a special bouquet of roses that she had picked from the ever-blooming rose garden beside the sparkling stream.

"Why thank you, my dear. What a special token of your love for me. I have a special gift to give you too. I wanted to save it for your eighteenth birthday. But now, I'd like you to have it."

The dragon walked over to the queen and gave a long, slow bow. "The phoenix is now Eiliope's. Its powers will pass to her."

In that instant, the queen aged rapidly, almost as if the years dripped off of her. Her long, beautiful blonde hair became grey and wiry, and even her wrinkles had wrinkles.

Eiliope cried, "Noooooooooooooo! I don't want it anymore! I give back the phoenix! Don't! I give it back! Dragon, give the phoenix back to my mother!" Eiliope fell into a heap at the queen's feet and cried.

Before long, Naeltim, the sylph of the air, blew a warm magical wind into Queen Corraelis's face. She immediately grew younger, and the phoenix sang sweetly.

Eiliope was still on the floor, hunched over in a ball and crying a river of tears that turned into a river of emeralds and rubies. Startled, she scooped some off of the floor. Her mother's hand rested on her shoulder. Eiliope was afraid to look up, so she just put her hand over her mother's and felt her mother's smooth, beautiful skin. Princess Eiliope lifted her eyes and saw her mother standing before her, as beautiful as she had ever been.

"Mother!" Eiliope stood and fell into the arms of her mother as the phoenix sang sweetly.

ABUNDANCE

DID YOU KNOW

I don't know if I know
I know that I feel
I feel you in the wind on my cheek
The bird on that branch
And the rain on the roof of my car.
Because it is in the cosmic dance
That everything is finally revealed
And the secret is no more
Than a warbler peeking at my window
Singing its song
And, once again,
I don't know if I know
I know that I feel

November 7, 2019
Bloomfield, Connecticut

LUCE IN HAVEN

nce upon a time, in a deep dark cave, lived a cruel gnome who had forced a small, frail ferret to live in a dark box. Having been trapped inside the box for too many years to count, the poor ferret's eyes and spirit had gotten used to living in darkness. She was only released when the cruel gnome went hunting, and that was never for very long.

One day, after the cruel gnome left to fetch water at a nearby stream, a butterfly accidently flew through a crack in the rocks into the cruel gnome's cave. All the butterflies knew that the cave belonged to the gnome and was a dangerous place to be, but the butterfly didn't realize her mistake until it was too late. Once she was inside, the butterfly discovered the length and breadth of the darkness in the cave, and it made her heart sink. She fluttered and fluttered as she tried to escape, and she fluttered even faster and more furiously after she saw that the gnome had captured and pinned her brother and sister butterflies to a board that he'd mounted on his kitchen wall.

She became very frightened and confused at the sight of the pinned butterflies. Overwhelmed with terror and not knowing what to do, she fluttered her way through the slats of a very dark closet inside the cave instead of escaping. She sunk to the ground and took shelter on top of a box that was sitting on the floor of the closet. Suddenly, the cardboard under her feet shuddered. At once, she scattered, flying around the closet and hitting the gnome's old, ragged clothes before she landed on top of the box again and collapsed from exhaustion.

In that moment of complete and total silence, the butterfly heard a slight whimper. Whimpers are much worse than cries. Cries are loud and proud. Whimpers usually hold the ultimate secret sadness, which is the most awful kind of sadness, as it always occurs in the dark.

When the butterfly heard the whimper, she turned to the box and asked in her butterfly voice, impossible for gnomes and ordinary people to hear, "Hello? Is someone in there?"

The ferret didn't know what to say because no one had ever asked her anything before. In fact, she was too afraid to speak. Yet the small, sweet voice of the butterfly made her feel warm inside and shone a light into her sad heart. Suddenly, in the space of time it took the butterfly to ask her very important question, the ferret decided to answer and opened her mouth.

"Yessssss." This was all the ferret could manage to say because, you see, when you are not allowed to speak for a very long time, you can lose the ability to say what's needed most.

"Are you a . . ." the butterfly choked up before continuing, ". . . butterfly?" The thought so horrified the butterfly that she nearly fell off the box, because all she could think about was the sight of her brothers and sisters hanging from pins near the cruel gnome's cupboard in the kitchen.

"I don't know what I am," the ferret said. "No one has ever told me."

The butterfly tried with all her might to take the top off the box, but for all her fluttering and all her will, it was too heavy for her to lift with her tiny butterfly feet.

The butterfly landed on the top of the box again and said, "We have to get you out of here. But I'm not powerful enough to lift the lid of this box all by myself, and we have very little time. Can you get out of the box yourself?"

Again, there was a moment of total silence.

Could the ferret? Would the ferret?

Way down inside the box, the ferret had crept into a corner and started shaking.

The box underneath the butterfly's little butterfly feet shook. The butterfly trembled with fear at the creature's silence, just as she had at the sight of her brothers and sisters pinned to the cruel gnome's wall.

"Miss whoever-you-are, we have very little time. The cruel gnome will be back soon, I should think."

The box shook even more.

"I want to help you get out of here," the butterfly said, just as the door to the closet opened.

At the sound of the word "help," the ferret's heart filled with light yet again. The offer spoke into the darkness of the ferret's sadness and awakened her heart to the promise of friendship, something the little ferret had never known.

At the sound of the thuds from the gnome's heavy, booted feet, the ferret stopped shaking.

"Are you still there?" the ferret asked the butterfly.

"Yessssss," the butterfly said, who was more frightened than the ferret now.

All of a sudden, Naeltim, the sylph of the air, blew so hard that the earth trembled. The butterfly experienced a terrible earthquake and the top of the box exploded, sending the butterfly flying high to the top of the closet.

Far below, she saw the ferret slither out of the box. And before she knew it, the closet door flew open and the little ferret charged out of the cave and all the way down to the stream where the butterfly bushes grew and sat below the very bush where the butterfly lived. The butterfly flew quickly after the ferret, trying to follow as best she could, but butterflies can't fly nearly as fast as frightened, hopeful ferrets can run when they are looking for safety.As the butterfly finally caught up to the ferret, she asked, "What's your name?"

"I don't have a name," the ferret replied.

"I'll call you Luce," the butterfly said. "It's Italian and means *light*. Always remember to let your light shine."

They decided it would be best for Luce to hide at the base of one of the butterfly bushes until her eyes got stronger, because the light of the sun was too bright for her tiny eyes since she'd spent so long in the dark box. The ferret sat at the base of the butterfly's home for nearly a week, adjusting to life in the sun.

On one sunny summer day, the ferret enjoyed her first sunbath on a very large rock by the stream. A fisherman across the river saw the ferret and thought she was the most beautiful ferret he'd ever seen. He put down his creel full of fish and his fishing reel and waded across the river to speak to the ferret.

"*Come ti chiami?*" he asked, which means "what is your name?" in Italian.

The ferret stretched because she'd just awoken from a very long, sweet dream. Life beside the river had been very pleasant and had left the dark memories of the cruel gnome behind.

"*Mi chiamo Luce,*" the ferret said. Animals can speak every language on Earth, unlike humans, so it's very easy for animals to understand the people of the world. And the ferret could tell, even with her tiny eyes that were still not quite used to the light, that this man had fallen in love with her just as she had with him.

He scooped up Luce in his hands and, after she said goodbye to her first friend, the butterfly, he took her to his home just outside of Milan. Luce turned out to be the most loving, sweetest ferret in the world, and she made many ferret friends at her new home. She even had her own blanket and a wonderful little cave of her own, made out of clean, fresh-smelling rags.

One day, the fisherman took Luce to Haven, a safe place filled with other animals he had rescued and many more the villagers had saved from the same darkness Luce had experienced her entire life. She became fast friends with the animals there. Different animals have no trouble speaking each other's language, unlike humans from different places.

Luce liked to check in on the animals, and because she was such an excellent communicator, she was given the very important job of introducing the new animals that arrived at Haven to the rest of the animals there. She loved helping the new, frightened animals find their light and their voice. Many of them were, as she once was, frightened in the darkness and unable to speak.

When another ferret, just like her, had been brought to Haven, not by the fisherman but by a local seamstress, Luce felt even more joyful. The seamstress discovered that a laboratory had tested cosmetics on the ferret. Her fur was horribly splotchy, and she cowered in the corner of Haven's reception area, just as Luce had once cowered in the corner of her box.

"What's your name?" Luce asked the frightened ferret.The ferret pointed to the brand on her skin. "I'm number thirty-three," she said.

The darkness almost colored Luce's world again. In a single second, all her light almost drained out of her beautiful body. But she took a big breath and said, "Thirty-three isn't a name, silly. I will give you a name. From now on your name is Sole; it means sun!"

Suddenly the ferret stopped shivering and left the corner of the reception area.

"I like the sound of Sole," she said.

Luce took Sole's paw. "I have some animals who can't wait to meet you," she said.

They went off to the barn first. They played tag and ran down a few hills to get there. When they walked in the barn, they met a donkey named Sophia. The owners of Haven had saved her from the slaughterhouse. The two ferrets also met Bianchina the cow. A citizen had found her roaming the streets of Catania and discovered her owner had schemed to sell her to a slaughterhouse.

Everyone who met Sole all wanted to know one thing: What had happened to her?

Sole didn't know how to begin. She trembled with all the new eyes staring at her, even though they were kind eyes. Bad things can be difficult to talk about just because it's hard to find the right words sometimes.

"I had a hard time talking about what happened to me, too," Luce said. "Would it help to know what happened to me?"

Sole nodded.

"Well, a cruel gnome had locked me up in a small wooden box and I escaped when he went hunting. Only then did I get to see the light of the sun."

Miriam the pregnant dog chimed in. "The owners of Haven rescued me just a few months ago. I almost suffocated because the people who owned me attached heavy weights to my collar so I wouldn't run away. They wanted to sell my puppies to a laboratory, and I would never have seen them again."

Mango the ostrich screeched, "My owner raised me to sell my beautiful and colorful feathers!"

Agatha the sheep baah'd, "My owners raised me for my wool."

Mindy, a shy rabbit, whispered, "My keepers wanted my Angora fur. It hurt terribly when they shaved it off." A tear left her eye.

"I know what you mean," Sole said. She didn't have to say anything more. Her patches of shaved and scraggly fur did all the talking. "The laboratory rubbed different chemicals on me, and now I fear I will never be furry again."

The animals gathered around Sole bowed their heads. They all knew what it was like to heal after so much pain.

"Sole, look around this beautiful land," Luce said.

Sole picked her head up and stared at the gorgeous hillsides where the wind blew over fields of wheat growing in the summer sun, and she observed the scraggly vineyard branches as they clung to wires in the orchard. She breathed in the earth's scent.

"All of this has been growing just for you," Luce said. "It's been preparing to meet and provide for you. For a long time, the owners of Haven worked hard to rescue and accommodate all the beautiful animals who, little by little, found their way here and now call it home."

"All this for me?" Sole said.

"For you," Bianchina the cow said.

"A long time ago, a greedy person lived on the property," Luce explained. "He was a person who didn't care about the animals or the land and only cared about money. One day, the greedy person became sick and left this land behind. The land longed to help creatures great and small to provide a safe home for them so they wouldn't have to suffer ever again. Caring and loving people now take care of Haven, making sure that it stays safe and protected forever."

Many months later, when the grapes were heavy on the vine and the owners had picked the olives and pressed them, Sole helped Luce at the petting zoo where little kids learned about their stories and got to pet their fur. Sole's fur had grown thick and luscious, and she was the most popular animal at the petting zoo.

PATIENCE

WILD HORSES

It's painful

It's the reflection that is slowly killing my soul.

It's a fantastic feeling to fly free

With that breeze on my cheek

And the exhilaration of adventure again.

The cycle has returned

Where I need to pause and reflect.

Running around in circles

Doing the same thing

Over and over

Hoping that the pain will one day subside.

The desire to burst

Burst into the new me

Burst into the old me

Running like a wild horse

With and against the wind.

November 21, 2019
Boulder, Colorado

RAPID SPARKLE'S WILD RIDE

 large circus had just arrived in Longwhisper Haunt, a place where children lived with their families in big concrete houses, and where not a leaf grew or an animal roamed. The only time the citizens of Longwhisper Haunt saw any animals at all was when the circus came to town, once a year on Halloween.

The circus of misfits and bandits treated their animals poorly. Many of the exotic animals had been trapped from the mountain range beyond the concrete wall of the Haunt and from other faraway lands.

On the day the circus came to town in Longwhisper Haunt, old Hector the mustang sang his own special song to while away the hours while he was chained to an old, weathered wooden fence in a makeshift stable at the back of the circus. He watched as the misfits and bandits set about raising the circus tent and securing the ticket booth.

He would perform later that night and knew everything had to be perfect. If it was not, the misfits and bandits would not give him any slop to eat for dinner. So he sang to keep the fear and pain away. He dreamed of performing, wearing his favorite dress of silver and gold and a special diamond crown that made him dream of far-off lands, where horses were royalty and lived in stables on vast grasslands—the lands he remembered from his youth.

Wearing the dress and performing in front of the crowd was the only time Hector felt special. So until the misfits and bandits came to unshackle him, he filled his mind with dreams of freedom and of his next performance. Hector sang and reminisced about being a little colt and running wild and free on the grasslands of Stormy Range with his family of wild horses.

Stormy Range was not far from Longwhisper Haunt, and was a place where the flowers bloomed every springtime and snow blanketed the fields every winter. Rapid Sparkle the mustang lived there with his fellow wild horses. He knew nothing of Longwhisper Haunt, having never climbed over the Continental Divide that separated the Haunt from his home in Stormy Range. He never wanted to leave his beautiful pastures and life of freedom, so he never went looking for anything else. His journeys were wild, fast, and fun, but he never travelled very far.

On the day that Hector was chained to the old wooden fence, Rapid Sparkle, who was born on the open range of the Wild West, galloped to Stormy Range's foraging area at the mouth of a canyon that sliced through the vast Continental Divide. That day he made new friends with some new mustangs and their families.

"On the other side of that ridge is Longwhisper Haunt," one of Rapid Sparkle's new friends said with a look of fear in his eyes.

Rapid Sparkle took a long look at the entrance to the canyon and then looked back at his new friend. "What scares you so about Longwhisper Haunt? What are you afraid of?" Rapid Sparkle replied.

But the little mustang only had this to say: "Stay far, far away from Longwhisper Haunt."

At the end of their foraging and playing, Rapid Sparkle and his new friends were exhausted from their wild running and needed some rest. First, they traveled to the river where they all took cool, long drinks.

"Thank you," Rapid Sparkle said to the river.

Once the mustangs had gotten their fill of water, they cantered to the rolling grasslands close to the open canyon and lay in comfy mounds of soft, fluffy hay. Just-harvested carrots were strewn on the ground, just as they were every night on Stormy Range. Mustangs who lived there never had to worry about going hungry.

"Thank you," Rapid Sparkle said to the hay and the carrots. He remembered traveling over the wild western prairies when he was young, yet he was never afraid of bandits or starving. It seemed that the things he needed always came to him. He felt content in his happy life on the range, settled into the hay and rested peacefully.

Meanwhile, no misfit or bandit had released Hector from his shackles. Hours and hours and hours went by and Hector became sad, hungry, thirsty, and afraid. Whenever he saw a misfit or a bandit, he neighed as loud as he could to get their attention, but to no avail. He tried to pace, but his shackles kept him bound. He tried to whinny to get more attention, but he seemed invisible. As he began to lose his mind, he started to sing an old song from when he was just a tiny colt,

"Delightful Drums on the Range":

The sight of the delightful range will always be heaven to me . . .

A range that will never leave my heart no matter where I roam, but still . . .

Take me back home. Home on the range.

Far away, over the concrete wall and through the canyon of the mountainous range, Rapid woke up in the hay, his belly full of carrots. Hector's voice carried over the mountains and through the canyon. Rapid started singing along to "Delightful Drums from the Range." He had sung it with his best friend on the wild western plains when they were just colts.

And although Rapid hadn't sung the song or sung at all in a very long time, he remembered every word. He rose from the hay, shook the sleep off, and sang loud and proud:

The range is where my heart should always be . . .
Delightful drums forever . . .

And soon, even though Hector and Rapid were miles and miles and miles apart, Rapid's voice reached Hector, traveling on a strong breeze that suddenly threw around the stale hay on the floor of the shabby stable where Hector and the other captive animals were confined. Hector was startled to be singing this long-distance duet. He recognized the voice but couldn't place where he'd heard it before. Overwhelmed, he stopped singing and sat back on his hard shackles, allowing the lyrics and Rapid's voice to wash over him, mouthing each word silently:

The range is where my heart should always be . . .
Delightful drums forever . . .

A feeling of contentment, unlike anything Hector had known before, brought him back to life despite all the ways he'd died a little every day since his capture. It was like he'd been painted in wonder and joy and he no longer felt alone for the first time in a very long time. No one had sung with him since the days he'd been a wild colt, running free on the plains of the Wild West. Hector longed to know the identity of the one who had once again put a beautiful smile on his face and joy in his heart.

Thrilled beyond measure, Hector cried out, "Who are you? Who is singing with me?"

The Tall Man walked over the back of the circus grounds, where Hector was, and used the heel of his very shiny black shoe to kick Hector's tail.

"Be quiet! Esampu the Elephant Enchantress is in the center ring!" the Tall Man said.

Hector's body hurt from the kick, and he was so thirsty now that he could barely see. The joy he'd felt at the sound of Rapid's voice drained out of him, and he sunk back down into the dirt along with all the other animals who were shackled there. But Hector never performed that night, and his dreams of wearing his gold and silver dress with the diamond crown turned into a nightmare of hunger, thirst, and pain. He watched as Esampu the elephant hobbled back to her cage. She collapsed in a heap. They fell asleep staring at each other. Her beautiful crown of diamonds and rubies dazzled Hector into dreamland.

The next day, Hector awakened to the sound of horses' hooves clomping on the concrete pavement. *Clomp-clomp, clomp-clomp.* Hector looked everywhere. He was the only horse in the circus, and yet, there were the sound of horse hooves. Hector grew more and more excited and stood up quickly to try and catch sight of the mystery horse. But when he got to his feet, his wobbly legs made him stumble. It took all his strength to stand again. But still, he couldn't see much of the circus grounds from the makeshift stable at the back of the circus. It was at this moment that the clowns brought over some slop for the animals, a collection of llamas, zebras, and camels.

As Hector ate the slimy scraps, a stew that the Tall Man had forced the Human Cannonball to make from discarded garbage that the misfits and bandits had dined on the night before, Hector dreamed of the carrots he had once eaten on the range and the joy he had felt, however briefly, when he'd heard the voice that had sung with him the night before.

It must have been a dream, Hector thought. *There is no way that such a feeling of joy could ever be part of my reality.*

Hector could hardly stomach the slop that he was forced to eat. He ate and ate, and although his belly was full, his head ached from a lack of proper nutrition. Former wild mustangs forced into a life of circus tricks needed much more than leftover slop and kicks in the tail to perform the way the Tall Man demanded.

Hector's heart leaped at the sound of keys clanging on his shackles. The Human Cannonball freed him from his prison. One by one, each of the zebras, llamas, and camels were unshackled too. They were hosed off by the bandits and left to stand in the sun until, one by one, they entered the wardrobe tent. Hector watched happy families stream into the main circus tent as he waited his turn. Still, he heard the *clomp-clomp, clomp-clomp* of horse hooves.

When it was Hector's turn, he walked into the wardrobe tent and saw for the first time in a very long time his precious dress of silver and gold and his special diamond crown. A few bandits strapped on Hector's large saddle and then fastened his silver and gold dress to it before snapping his tiara down around his ears. Then the Hydra Lady brought Hector out into the afternoon light, which nearly blinded Hector. His eyes weren't as good as they used to be.

The large, seven-foot-tall Hydra Lady brought him over to the tall white ladder that she used to mount him before every show. The band in the circus tent played louder and louder—Hector's cue that they would be the next act. Hector cringed at the idea of the Hydra Lady's weight on his back again. With as weak and sick as he felt, he thought that this time his back would certainly break. With each rung that the Hydra Lady mounted, higher and higher, Hector's head sunk lower and lower. He prepared himself for the thud of her dropping into his saddle and the intense agony of each *clomp-clomp* step toting her around the tent to the laughs of small children. But instead of feeling the thud of the Hydra Lady in his saddle, he once again heard *clomp-clomp, clomp-clomp, clomp-clomp, clomp-clomp*!

Rapid Sparkle galloped from his hiding place behind the dilapidated, makeshift stable at the back of the circus, rounded the ladder, and reared up in front of Hector. Just as the Hydra Lady was about to step off the ladder to descend on Hector's back, Hector broke free from his weary workhorse trance to gallop along with Rapid. The Hydra Lady landed on the ground, yelling and complaining. She wasn't in pain because all of her weight acted like a cushion.

Together, Hector and Rapid galloped to the iron fence that encircled the circus grounds. But before Rapid could kick down the gate that separated them from the outside world and the promise of freedom at Stormy Range, Hector screamed, "Wait! We can't leave without Esampu the Enchantress!"

Big, wide-eyed Esampu stared in trepidation at Hector and Sparkle as they made their way back to her cage. Hector felt a renewed energy rise inside of him, and he reared up high to kick down the bars of Esampu's cage. She escaped quickly and used her large snout to give Hector a hug. Together, Rapid, Esampu, and Hector tore down the circus gate. They galloped out of the concrete city and through the vast canyon in the mountain range, up and up all the way to the highest elevations of Stormy Range, singing:

Travel this way, range is your land . . .

We shall travel again to the beat of our drums . . .

Once they reached Stormy Range, Rapid and Hector played all the games they used to play when they were young mustangs. Esampu enjoyed sunning herself in the vast grasslands. Hector also played with many of his old friends that he remembered from before. They ate juicy tall grass, and at night when they settled down in the soft hay and looked at the stars, Hector, Esampu, and Rapid ate all the fresh carrots they wanted. To this day, you can hear the voices of Hector and Rapid on the winds of the prairie singing new songs.

FREEDOM

NOISES

Why am I still here
When I so want to leave
And never look back?
It snowed again, and I am trapped.
Crying won't help
When all I need is to sit quiet
And reflect.

November 27, 2019
Boulder, Colorado

DORIS IN THE GREEN AND THE BATS

oris-in-the-Green was a very large woodland fairy who lived in her lair at the edge of Humber Pike. Compared to her peers, who were tiny fairies no bigger than a Southern California hummingbird, Doris was SO big that she could barely fit in her lair. Doris was as big as a duck. She even walked like a duck, and she kind of looked like a pixie. Her long, fine, carrot-colored hair framed eyes as green as the greenest frog, and her silvery, shimmering wings were paper thin.

Because of her gregarious nature, she threw out hilarious jokes. Since all the fairies in the land loved to laugh more than anything, she became very popular and got invited to all the best parties. Fairies are funny and fun-loving, and funny-looking Doris was the best storyteller of them all. She also loved sweet butter and honey cake, and she was an expert at baking for herself and her family and friends. Her friend the canary visited her outside of her kitchen window every day to keep her company as she baked her favorite cakes.

Each time she left her lair in search of milk and the best honey to make her favorite cake, she had to squeeze through the entrance of her lair. It took her a long time to fit her big, chunky body through the little arched doorway. And when she returned with all her goodies, she often carried so many supplies that she tumbled over and dropped everything. She wasn't fairy graceful and lost her balance easily. But she embraced her goofiness. It gave her great joy to bake her favorite cakes for her family and friends and make fairies laugh because fairies' laughter lifted the spirits of everyone in the woodland. When everyone was happy, the sun felt warmer and the colors of the wood glowed brighter.

Still, she secretly wished she wasn't so clumsy. She felt out of place, even though she was the highlight of every party. See, there's a difference between people who love you and laugh with you and those who laugh at you. The experience of hearing fairies mutter jokes under their breath about her hopelessly thin, delicate wings made Doris shrink inside. Slowly, her jovial nature began to slip away.

This began in small ways on the day Doris realized that her plump nature kept her from exercising her wings. Because she didn't exercise them, her wings became paper thin, although they were still very exquisite. She had the silkiest, most silvery wings of any fairy in Humber Pike. She tried to fly, but every time she took to the air, she fell back down to the earth—hard! She couldn't even flutter her wings. That's why she became the master baker and storyteller in Humber Pike instead. She couldn't do what every other fairy could.

Just when she started to question why she'd even been born a fairy at all, Doris became the most important fairy who ever lived. You see, before the events in this story took place, fairies spent their days flying in and out of their own lairs, which they had decorated according to their own senses of style. It was all the rage to have the most up-to-date artwork on the walls of their lairs and the most efficient kitchen appliances in their tiny kitchens. But they spent most of their days playing jokes on the woodland animals, like the white-tailed deer, coyotes, red foxes, squirrels, porcupines, and beavers. Because that's what fairies do; they lift spirits through their folly. When they had gotten their fill of belly laughs, they swiftly flew home to their own lairs.

But in an odd twist of fate, one day Doris opened her door after baking her favorite honey cakes, and every fairy in the land flew inside her house.

"Goodness! What on earth is going on!" Doris exclaimed. She thought they might be playing a joke on her.

And in their teeny-tiny voices, the fairies said, "We're afraid of the outside world! We don't want to live alone anymore. We all want to live together here with you!"

"Well, whatever made you feel this way?" Doris said. "The sun is still shining, and the wood is still as it always was. Nothing has changed."

"We heard there are fairy-catchers out there who are looking for the funniest fairies in all the land," a fairy said.

Doris dropped her honey cake.

"What? Why would they want to trap funny fairies? There must be some kind of misunderstanding," Doris said.

"No, it gets worse! There are people who are harvesting the wings of fairies to use in special potions . . . I forget what they call these creatures . . ." another fairy said.

"I think they called them witches . . ." a fairy chimed in.

As they buzzed around in fear, they almost knocked down her not-up-to-date paintings off the wall.

So the fairies abandoned their practice of living alone in their own teensy lairs with the most up-to-date artwork and the best kitchen appliances, because they became afraid of the outside world. They believed there was strength in numbers.

Because her cavernous lair instilled a sense of safety and she was able to always downplay serious situations, Doris's home became a shelter for all the fairies, and life became like one gigantic sleepover party. Since Doris didn't like housekeeping very much, her lair was messier than the lairs of the other fairies, and she didn't have the most up-to-date artwork or the latest in kitchen appliances. But those things didn't matter to the fairies anymore. They were happy to be together in their refuge from the outside world, where strange happenings occurred—inexplicable things like the disappearances of fellow fairies and the clipping of their wings.

One midsummer night, the fairies were sound asleep, wrapped up in their cozy little beds made of silky rainbow handkerchiefs—all except for Doris, who was awake. Because she was much larger than a normal fairy and wouldn't fit in a tiny bed, Doris needed a proper bed, specially installed for her on the wall of her lair by a wonderful gnome skilled in woodcraft. She had been sleeping under super-soft cotton rainbow sheets when a thunderstorm boomed throughout the woodland and all the fairies woke up.

After the heavy rain and thunder subsided, the fairies, who were used to occasional heavy summer rains, went back to a sound sleep. But then there was an even louder, more terrifying noise. They heard the flapping of wings! Many of the fairies flew onto the windowsill of Doris's lair to get a better look at the beasts. Because they had flown under cover of night, the fairies couldn't spot them, not even with their binoculars.

"No worries, ladies, it's probably just a bunch of bats trying to get free rent!" Doris said.

As the first rays of sun entered on the following day, it turned out that the lair's ceiling was chock-full of Doris-sized bats roosting on the ceiling! The fairies weren't the only creatures in the wood looking for a safe place to sleep. Scared of the thunderstorm, the bats had seen Doris's home and thought it was a wonderful place where they would be safe from the rain and thunder.

The fairies, who were used to playing jokes on the animals and then flying away, had never seen anything so weird! They were frightened by the bats and hid under their rainbow-print handkerchiefs, trembling. They couldn't play jokes and then fly away, because the bats were in THEIR lair! They didn't think any of this was funny at all! Because Doris was the funniest, most jolly fairy, and because it was her home, the bats didn't scare her like they did the other fairies. She sensed something must have scared the bats, and she knew that laughter was the best medicine for fear.

The bats' loud snores surprised Doris and made the fairies tremble even more. But Doris didn't care. It was her joy to provide a safe place for the bats, and since she wasn't much of a housekeeper, she didn't mind the mess they made.

When morning came, she began her day as she always had, baking honey cakes as the bats snored away. While she happily baked her twenty-one cakes—sixteen for her family and friends and five for herself—she sang her happy, silly songs and looked up toward the ceiling. She noticed the bats were still shaking from fear. So were the fairies.

As she stirred her batter, Doris conjured up a brilliant idea, which she confided to the little canary that visited outside her window while she baked her cakes.

"How about I set up a honey cake and sweet butter party for everyone? I'm sure that will be the cure-all. I have enough honey and butter to make enough sweet cakes for everyone, including the bats. The bats will know that they are safe here, and my fairy family will know that there is no reason to fly away from them. We will all enjoy our cakes together and become friends."

The canary sang sweetly, and Doris went to work.

She baked the cakes faster than she thought she would, and so she had time leftover to decorate her little fairy home with lots of streamers and little fairy party poppers and horns, the kind that crinkle and roll out long when you blow on them. And when the fairies finally left their tiny cozy little beds made of silky rainbow handkerchiefs, they flew around Doris's house all excited. They couldn't wait to eat their honey cakes.

"This is the kindest thing anyone has ever done for me!" one fairy said with a smile so big, well big for a fairy, that it melted Doris's enormous heart.

The fluttering of fairy wings and party horns woke up the bats. They couldn't fall back to sleep because of the fabulous fragrance of Doris's honey cakes. They fluttered down off the rafters of Doris's home.

"These are for you!" Doris said.

"For us?" the bats said.

"Yes, they're not juicy bugs, but it's what fairies like to eat. Do you think you'd like to try some?"

A few of the bats huddled together. They couldn't stop salivating because all they had eaten for ever and ever were little bugs. And because Doris knew this, the canary had helped her put some crunchy bugs inside their honey cakes.

So when they bit down on their cakes, they had a tasty surprise.

"These cakes are marvelous! Thank you so much!" a bat said. But then the bat couldn't open his mouth for a while, and the fairies started laughing.

Doris had put a little extra honey in there too, so the bats couldn't speak for a short time after they ate their cakes. Her lair became very, very quiet indeed while the honey dissolved in the bats' mouths. Then the whole lair filled up with belly laughter. The belly laughter of bats and fairies is unlike any sound you've ever heard, shrill and sweet. And the fairies had never laughed so hard in all their lives because it was their custom to dream up jokes, play them, and then fly away. This was the first joke they had witnessed. So, they had the impact of not just laughing at the thought of the joke, but seeing it happen in front of them. Some of them liked it so much that they started thinking they wouldn't fly away.

"So, what did you put in that cake?" the bat said, still tearing up from laughing so hard.

"A secret ingredient," Doris said.

Before long, the fairies had swept away the bats' mess, and the bats made the fairies' little rainbow-handkerchief beds. When the bats saw how beautiful the daytime was, filled with gorgeous blooming flowers and soft green meadows, they offered to take the fairies for piggy-back rides through the woodland. Naeltim, the sylph of the air, gave them the perfect breeze to fly on.

From that time on, the bats kept watch over the fairies at night, and neither the bats nor the fairies had anything to fear. The bats protected the fairies at night, swooping down to scare away anyone who threatened to clip their wings. And the fairies made the bats laugh during every thunderstorm. And Doris never questioned why she was born a fairy ever again.

ORIGINALITY

PEACE

Horses running

Infinite pastures

Behind the home we once both inhabited

Never ending horizons

Where mountains meet the sky

Openness as vast as the cosmos

And the silence and peace of returning Home

**December 28, 2019
Boulder, Colorado**

THE STAR BOAT
AND THE
THREE LOST MEN

nce upon a time, in a far, far away galaxy, there lived a boy who sat on a moon. He was the Master Keeper of the Universe. Wise beyond his years, he looked very small, but he possessed a loving spirit the size of the entire universe, and so the universe had delegated the great duty of balancing love through the galaxies.

This was not an easy task. You see, people often hide their love. It would have been easy if the boy could have used his hearing alone to know the hearts of all beings. But because people don't say they love each other and mean it, very often the boy had to look at their actions to discern the truth. And, when love wasn't present, the boy needed to balance the lives of people who had poured too much love into life so they would receive love instead.

What does a boy know of love? In this matter, you'd be surprised. For who can better see the truth of the world than a child? And who can better know the joy of the world? The universe was pleased with its choice of the boy, for it never makes a mistake.

Twice a year—galaxy years are much, much shorter than our own—the boy would lead a journey through the stars for all the people who wanted to learn more about compassion and empathy. The boy and his crew ran this experience with great efficiency. All the seekers were assigned an embarkation time, but debarkation depended only on when they had learned their lesson. At their allotted embarkation time, seekers would set sail upon the Star Boat.

While it was the journey of a lifetime, it wasn't for the faint of heart. The boy took the helm and captained the seekers on a passage through the stars, taking them to witness scenes of poverty and greed, wars and famine, terrible destruction, and even death. This often made the seekers uncomfortable with the truths of their worlds and forced them to lift the veils of ignorance and confusion that they had been wearing. During this difficult and at times disheartening process, their hard hearts softened. It is true that seas are calmest before a great storm. And people, just like the seas, have a false sense of calm before the tempest hits. The boy taught the seekers how to stay calm in savage seas and how to find a center of their own boats: their hearts. They took time with him to understand their own hearts and their own intentions. But at the beginning of their journeys, none of the seekers knew the agony of what they would experience during their journey.

The boy captained the Star Boat and sailed it through the galaxy, navigating it to the brightest star in the universe, where he'd find the next group of new seekers at their allotted boarding time. One beautiful starry night, the skies were so wide and filled with stars that the new passengers stood in awe of such majestic beauty. Husbands and wives and their children waited in line for the boy, all giggly with the anticipation of the Star Boat's arrival and that it was finally their turn to take a journey. For it was known far and wide throughout the universe that the people who came back from the journey would go on to do great deeds.

The spectacle of the boy sailing the Star Boat brought chills to those seekers gathered on the docks. They saw a flash of light in the sky, and then a slow-burning star landed on the sea swells in front of their eyes. The indescribable beauty and power of the descent captivated the seeker crowd and left them speechless. In that silence, their hearts realized they all had lessons to learn. The red tide waters illuminated the bow of the ship so that it appeared to glow with the light of human kindness at its approach. The waves appeared painted with the warmest light on the darkest of nights and reflected onto the boat's wooden gunnels. A gentle breeze brought by Naeltim, the sylph of the air, gently floated the Star Boat up to the dock. Then the First Mate let down a gangplank.

Instinct told the seekers to board and so, one by one, they walked up the gangplank and then stepped onto the deck of the Star Boat, a little unsure of their steps before they descended steep stairs into the hold. The boat appeared so much bigger on the inside than it did on the outside; some would say it was cavernous.

Slowly they settled into their cozy cabins, which had cozy beds and a small lamp on each nightstand. The staterooms had a porthole and a little bell in the shape of a fairy for seekers to ring in case of emergency. A seasoned crew prepared meals in the galley, and delivered the delectable food each day and night in little baskets at appointed times.

It was customary for each day to begin with the First Mate giving a small lecture about the world's issues most in need of compassion and empathy in the main salon, and afterward the seekers would pick the experience they wanted to observe. There were two rules they needed to abide by: be present and observe without finding a solution, or worse yet, turning away. And they could only ask one question of the people who they were observing at each port.

"The goal is to learn as much as possible about the situation at hand. You must see it all. Then, and only then, will you learn compassion and empathy," the First Mate said.

The seekers voyaged from unique experience to unique experience until they learned their own specific lesson. When they had learned that lesson, they disembarked from the Star

Boat and returned to their homes to put into practice all the wisdom they had learned.

Wrinkle was a seeker who desperately wanted to learn about compassion so he could return home and take action to help those around him. But he'd become an angry man, embittered by losing all the ones he'd loved. He suffered from the worst pain known in this life—that of a broken heart. When Wrinkle reported for his voyage on the Star Boat, the boy learned that the man's fate would have been to sink into a deep black hole from which he would never have returned.

Often fate gives the gift of despair to the people who shine the brightest. For, without it, they would never be truly called to do the work the universe has given them to do. Since the universe always uses suffering as a learning tool, it always uses suffering for good. And that's what happened the day Wrinkle boarded the Star Boat and set sail.

"There are many people in this world who know the key to happiness," the First Mate said that morning to the new seekers. "They know that happiness can't rely on the right relationship, or on certain important objects. They have found something mysterious, a quality beyond description."

"I want to discover the meaning of happiness," Wrinkle said.

"Then you may benefit from the scenes at any of the ports we visit," the First Mate said.

They sailed into many ports of call. Wrinkle disembarked at the bleakest among them, a place called Ravaged City, to discover the mysterious quality he hadn't stopped obsessing over ever since the First Mate's briefing. He toured sections of Ravaged City and saw people with little food, little shelter, and no work, yet they smiled the most beautiful smiles.

Many had lost loved ones in more heartbreaking ways than Wrinkle could have possibly imagined, yet the citizens never lost their happiness. Wrinkle visited them day after day after day, hypnotized by their happy ways. He knew the rules. And this caused him agony as he sat in silence and watched them play, laugh, and sing. He had his eye on a man with a brilliant, nearly toothless smile, very similar to Wrinkle in age. The old man wore ripped clothes and always held the hand of his beloved.

Wrinkle was dying of curiosity and could no longer sit on the sidelines. So many questions ran through Winkle's mind. Finally, he walked up to the man with the brilliant, nearly toothless smile, and asked, "What do you do when you can't smile?"

The old man replied, "I sing."

Another passenger on board the Star Boat, Root, was a greedy man. Money had been his best friend for years, and so he had no friends. He told the First Mate that he wanted to learn how to share. So, every day Root disembarked and traveled to a nearby school, where children were learning how to build a water well for their village. Before construction had begun on the well, each girl in the village had walked many miles each day to get water from a local river. This heavy, burdensome task made it impossible for girls to go to school like their brothers. One day, the village elder learned how to build wells from a traveling scientist. Together, they drew up the plans for the well, and the entire village helped dig the ground and lay the pipes.

Root struggled to find the right question to ask. But when he saw a beautiful breath of a woman digging in the dirt, a woman so thin a gust of wind might blow her away, his question came naturally.

"How can I help?" Root asked.

She passed him a shovel.

The village constructed the well so that the girls could get the education they needed. The girls thanked the village for the gift and gave back to the village by having a mighty party for everyone who helped. The party gave Root the first feeling of family he'd ever known.

Shadow, another passenger on the Star Boat, was an apathetic man who had never discovered passion, and he wanted to experience what that meant before he died. He didn't know where to begin, so the boy instructed the First Mate to watch over him especially, as passions, when they are new, can often overtake us. No one was more surprised than the boy when one day Shadow came aboard the Star Boat dressed in a Flamenco outfit and danced a perfect Flamenco. He had bought the entire troop of dancers back to the ship with him, and together they entertained the crew and all the passengers.

It was one of the most magical nights aboard the Star Boat. The boy learned how to dance Flamenco too. Before the night was over, they had quite a few passengers who showed a natural ability to dance. And that was just what Shadow needed—a tribe of people who enjoyed the art of movement. When he reached the streets of Harbor Town, he finally discovered his true passion and his one question.

"Can you teach me?" Shadow asked.

People who knew how to how to let their feelings show through dance taught Shadow how to move and how every movement of the dance was tied to his emotions. That night in the local bodega, Shadow came out of his own shadow. He wiggled his angst away long into the night, and he never felt passionless again.

COMPASSION

I AM LAUGHING AGAIN

I feel you falling

I feel you returning home

Flying among those spaces

Crying for help is no more

The empty space that you once left

Is now replaced by serenity

And it's a whimsical story

Of peaceful laughter and ethereal hearts

flying around.

January 11, 2020
Kanab, Utah

PIPER'S MAGIC
JOURNEY

nce upon a time, there was a mutt named Piper. She was unremarkable in every way. She had matted dark-brown fur and a long, flea-bitten tail. No human wanted her. She had almost given up hope because human families had already abandoned her twice—once because she barked too much and the other because she'd gotten too old to hunt. Being abandoned twice in her life gave her a pain deep inside her heart. She never thought she'd ever be able to run away from that pain, no matter how hard she tried. Her story really isn't any different from that of a million other dogs on the planet. But Piper was very different in one special way. She was a brilliant storyteller.

Among the strays in her village, Rumor had it that Piper's stories could heal. And of all the tales she learned to spin, one seemed so extraordinarily wonderful that it not only eased the pain of her friends but of all the abused and stray animals within earshot.

It was an unbelievable story.

When Piper launched into one of her tales, the scene was always the same. Usually, after a night of driving rain, stray and abandoned dogs would huddle around a trash heap, many of them fighting for scraps. Some of them, weary of constantly fighting for their lives, laid down to die, their frames so thin and frail that their skin sagged off their bones. Piper would take her place at the top of a mound of trash, an old garbage can, or on an abandoned chair or couch on the side of a dangerous, rarely traveled street. She liked to sit up high above all the other dogs because she believed that would help her voice reach as many strays as possible.

She sat tall, imagining her story reaching the ears of those who'd been so desperate as to lie down and die out of sight, yet were still within reach of her voice. It was those desperate animals that she worried about most of all. Piper had nightmares about all the animals that didn't have the strength to go on. She knew that when their time had come, many would hide away and die alone.

Maybe my voice can make a difference for them. Maybe my voice can bring them back to life, Piper would tell herself as she told the unbelievable story.

"Not very long ago, just around the corner, two women met who had never met before," Piper began.

"One was a very old woman who had seen little of the world except her island home. And the other was a young lady who had traveled all over the world and only recently had journeyed very far to enjoy the tiny island home of the old woman."

"What were their names?" a scruffy dog asked, his throat so parched he could barely get the words out. A terrible drought that year meant there was precious little fresh water to drink.

"Angela and Nona," Piper said. "They dreamed of building a sanctuary for animals. A place where any animal would find food, shelter, and loving hands to pet and hug them."

There was a collective sigh at the thought of such a place, and the dogs that had laid down to die rolled over, a breath of life seeming to fill their lungs.

"Only, they didn't know what they were doing," Piper added.

A few of the animals laughed, but most of the animals' eyes became the size of saucers.

"Angela and Nona didn't think providing shelter to so many stray and abandoned animals would be easy, but they didn't think it would be so hard."

"What made it so hard?" a blind Chihuahua asked.

"Time after time after time they met terrible obstacles," Piper said.

"Like what kind of obstacles?" one stray asked.

"Well, the first one was just bumping into each other in the first place," Piper said. "They met because a pregnant dog was about to have babies."

Just then, Piper saw some neglected puppies scurry out of the garbage heap. A tear came to her eye.

"Let me go back to the beginning," Piper said. "A beautiful, happy-go-lucky shepherd-pit bull puppy was born with one ear up and one ear down, and she loved her life at the sanctuary that the two women built. She shared the sanctuary with her mommy, daddy, siblings, and hundreds and hundreds of other majestic animals at the Oasis."

"That sounds like the ultimate destination," a large bulldog chimed in.

"That sounds like heaven," the scruffy dog said.

"It sounds too good to be true," a skinny puppy said, shivering.

"But it is real! It happens every day!" Piper said. "But before she ended up in the gorgeous sanctuary, where her puppy-time was filled with endless days of playing and laughing, she suffered. The puppy had been rescued from a dumpster in rural Texas together with her other four siblings. Their rescuers transferred them to a wonderful place, far away from Texas, to a land of enchantment in Utah called the Sunrise Shelter. The shelter sat amongst sweeping vistas, and the puppy had never seen the likes of it. The chiseled, beautiful land was full of rocks, and the ancient beauty of the Utah desert captivated the one-ear-up-one-ear-down puppy."

"That's a marvelous story," the shaggy dog said.

"But it's not over yet. It's not even the best part!" Piper said. "Well, it's too bad, but the little puppy didn't meet any other dogs. So in a way, she was all alone except for her siblings—but she was just a puppy, so she didn't really know anything different."

"That's sad that the puppy was alone. Still, it would be nice to be in a beautiful place where I didn't have to fight for my food," a starving mutt said nervously with a pensive stare.

"That's exactly what the little puppy thought," Piper said.

"One day, the puppy met Angela, a jolly lady who rescued the young puppy for the third time. The puppy wasn't lonely anymore and she loved Angela deeply, at first sight. There were many reasons for that, but one of them was that Angela loved to travel. Together they took a long trip in Angela's car, and they traveled all the way to Angela's cute home in Colorado, which had a wonderful backyard full of sunshine and green grass. The puppy loved the green grass because she'd never seen it before, and it had the most amazing smell, especially just after the gardeners had mowed. Sometimes the puppy liked to snack on the moist, flavorful, freshly cut blades of grass."

All the strays had crept closer to Piper as she spoke of the lucky puppy. And before long, even the dogs with the skin hanging off their bones rose to their little doggy feet and sat up, hanging on Piper's every word.

"Not too long after that, the one-ear-up-and-one-ear-down puppy took another trip. This time it was a lengthy trip on an airplane! To a place called Italy," Piper said.

"Airplane? What's an airplane?" one dog with skin hanging off her bones asked.

"It's like a car that travels in the sky!" yelled a mutt in the front row.

The dog with skin hanging off her bones smiled.

"I loved to chase cars when I was healthy and happy," she said. She sank back down to lie in the dirt, dreaming about what it would be like to chase cars in the sky.

"It was there, far, far away in a place called Italy, that Angela met Nona, who kept many dogs in her house, both big and small. The puppy loved to play with all of them. She raced around the yard and smelled the sunshine, enjoying the feel and smell of the land after being cooped up on the airplane. The puppy had a grand time, but she always stayed within earshot of Angela and Nona so she could hear the two ladies' conversation, because they were talking about saving dogs and creating a refuge for them."

"A refuge?" one dog barked out.

"It's like a home, only better. It's a place where they can heal and eat and rest and play," Piper said.

"That seems like an enormous job," a shy Pekingese said.

"It was, and . . . oh, the places they visited! A sweet woman showed them the most beautiful place imaginable—a sprawling place of peace, tranquility, and absolute beauty, lined with fruit trees and crowned with vast, open blue skies, where the most majestic birds soared and loved to sing and cheer up lost puppies. The island also had rolling hills and ancient ruins and extensive fields with nothing but grass for miles and miles. And there were rivers and bridges."

"I would love to drink from a river! Can we find one?" one stray asked.

"Rivers are very far away from us, but maybe someday!" Piper said.

"That place sounds like paradise to me, it doesn't even sound real," a Chihuahua said.

"And that's exactly what the puppy thought! But it wasn't easy to find this paradise. That was a real adventure. Angela, Nona, and the puppy always traveled by car on these winding island roads, and the puppy got to sit in the front seat!"

The dogs gasped.

"The front?!"

"Yes, the puppy traveled like a princess and always sat in the most comfortable seat. She even flew in airplanes, and not in the cargo hold, but the airplane's cabin, and she had beautiful collars specially made for her by a famous dog-collar maker in Belgium. Her mom also baked the puppy delicious dog cookies."

"Dog cookies?"

"Yes, they are treats that people give the pets they love," Piper said.

The dogs assembled at the garbage heap all sighed. Some licked their lips.

"People love their pets so much that they make them princesses and bake them cookies?" one dog said.

"Yes, they do. And that's not all! One day, when the princess puppy played in one particular spot, she discovered many other animals all around her, like cows and donkeys, grazing all over the beautiful, rolling hills. And she looked longingly at the beautiful trees and blue skies and felt a gentle breeze wash over her fur. 'One day, you too will live in such a beautiful place,' Angela whispered into the puppy's ear. The puppy's whole body was so filled with joy that she laid down in the tall, green grass and rolled around in the warmth of the sun. She wanted to remember this day forever."

Piper continued the story, saying that one afternoon Angela took the puppy for a walk on Nona's island home. The puppy loved running and playing along the beach and on the shores of the sparkling azure seas. The beautiful white sand beaches felt warm on her paws and made her feel warm inside too. The air had the sweet scent of oranges and the yummy scent of pasta and barbeque. And it all seemed like a dream.

But then, it turned into a nightmare. As Angela and the puppy rounded a corner of a little street, the puppy saw some dogs chained up to the back of one of the restaurant alleys. The puppy trembled in fear, and then she ran to free the other dogs.

"And then Angela said, 'It's okay, I want to rescue them too, just like I did with you.' Just then an ugly, mean old man came out to tighten the chains around the necks of the dogs. The chained dogs wailed as he clamped down hard on the chains. They were all sad and thought all was lost until they got a glance at the princess puppy, looking pampered and cared for," Piper said. "Angela made sure that the ugly man never hurt another puppy again. When the ugly man went to jail, the street slowly filled up with gorgeous animals and happy children, all playing with the puppies who needed homes."

Piper said that one day the puppy met her new best friend at an elderly dog shelter, a special place for very old dogs.

The oldest dog at the garbage heap, a mangy German shepherd, shakily rose to its feet. "You mean there's a place that takes care of old dogs too? I thought people who love their pets only loved puppies?"

"Yes, they do. And it was at this elderly dog shelter where the puppy met her very old best friend, an Australian shepherd named Black, who'd been rescued from the ugly man."

Piper then spoke about how the puppy, Black, Angela, and Nona overcame obstacle after obstacle to get the promised sanctuary built, the fulfillment of their dreams. Slowly they followed where the path led, never understanding how or why one door would always close just when their hearts had thought they found the perfect place.

But the perfect place finally came after a rigorous search and the heartbreak of many, many places that fell through. To find what they were looking for, Angela and Nona had to connect the dots, even when it didn't seem like there were any dots to connect! When they seemed to have run out of dots, they waited to see if some might reappear. The only thing Angela and Nona knew was what they wanted the sanctuary to be: a haven for abused and stray animals. They didn't focus on how it would happen and because of that, they stayed open to all possibilities even when it looked like they might never find the right place."

"Did they ever find their dream spot?" a dog shouted from the back of the crowd.

"Yes, they did," Piper said. "The sanctuary was always possible, even when all seemed lost. Their dream was like the trees in winter—it wasn't dead, just dormant; just waiting and preparing for the right time to come. And that's what Angela and Nona's search was like. All the hiccups and setbacks were preparing them for what was to come. Had they not been disappointed and disheartened, they never would have seen the beautiful opportunity that lay ahead—the perfect one, a place that would be much more than a sanctuary but also a place where children could come learn and play with the animals too."

"How do you know so much about this puppy? I've never heard this story before!" one of the dogs exclaimed.

"I once had a broken heart just like you. You see, that little puppy was me."

Just then, the puppies who had laid down to die around the garbage heap stumbled through a broken glass door and across the street to the garbage heap where Piper spoke. They stared at the old, one-ear-up-one-ear-down dog named Piper, and together they all bayed at the moon.

SERENDIPITY

IT'S STRANGE

Just as I knew nothing about you before you
arrived
I now know that your brief time here
Was just as brief as everything else
It's a speck in time
And time, I do not know
The honor of having been your Friend
Here on Earth
Means Love changes everything
And the swirling
And the laughter
Is just as very real
Now as when we were together.

January 11, 2020
Kanab, Utah

THE SECRET OF FRESH ROARING WATERS

nce upon a time, a very special river flowed through a large gorge in the ancient Middle East. The river sparkled blue in the sunshine and shimmered silver at moonrise. Its white waves rippled and curled with a freshness only found on the water. Its foam filled the river with oxygen, and its flow never ebbed. It sang as it journeyed along ancient cliff dwellings and rocky outcroppings. No other setting on Earth was the river's equal in beauty and tranquility. And only those who had been there before knew its location. So please don't go looking for it. It does no good to search for things you'll never find.

People along the riverbanks spent many a day watching people drift by on the most humble of rafts, the most ostentatious yachts, and the most antique junks. Inhabitants along the riverbank named the river Fresh Roaring Waters because of its awe-inspiring sounds and clean rushing water. The vitality of Fresh Roaring Waters inspired the locals and nourished their fields, and provided a constant source of well-being and beauty. The river taught many life lessons. All one needed to do was listen to the river and surrender to its power.

One beautiful day, three different people went to the river with their troubles. They all held too tightly to their own ideas and hadn't yet learned the art of being like water and flowing around the rocks that get in the way, like the river does. The rocks in their lives acted like dams and so their rivers of love, joy, and compassion—especially for themselves—had dried up.

Sometimes people don't want to change. They cease speaking or listening to humans. These were the people who came to Fresh Roaring Waters. They sat upon its banks and stared into the water, wondering why their struggles changed their countenances so totally that even those closest to them no longer recognized them.

One such boy sat at the banks of the beautiful blue river. He had nowhere else to turn. Fresh Roaring Waters gave him an unusual peace and a tranquility he'd never experienced before. He laid his sword down and rested on a windblown dune along the riverbank, possibly the most beautiful spot he'd ever seen in the world.

He was the son of a famous slain warrior, and his father's precious sword was all the boy really had of his father. The sword was just as powerful as it was beautiful, and the boy was afraid of learning how to use it. As he drifted off to sleep, he heard a voice.

"I will never leave you," the voice said.

The boy's grandparents had raised him to be fearful of all the world. They told him life was like a chess game, and he needed to always stay two moves ahead. Since he had no head for strategy, he had never learned how to use the sword because he knew he'd never measure up to his legendary warrior father.

In the boy's dream, the river invited the boy onto an enchanted boat that stopped at each of the riverside towns. Naeltim, the sylph of the air, blew fair winds to push the riverboat along. During this trip, the boy saw how other warrior boys learned to become strong—through trial and error and through perseverance. They practiced, fell down, and always got back up again. As the river took him on the journey, the boy lost his fear and self-doubt. He started looking at his sword as something to experience and not to master. He let go of feeling like he had to be the perfect warrior and instead became the unique warrior he knew how to be.

"Go with the flow," the river said.

When the boy woke up, the river's soothing words penetrated his spirit. He shook his head and then stared at the river; the dream seemed so real. *Was it a dream?* he wondered. The boy picked up his father's ancient sword with newfound authority and practiced his battle moves along the riverbank. He darted here and crisscrossed his footwork there, just like great warriors. Once his moves flowed perfectly, he stopped to take one last look at the river.

Fresh Roaring Waters whispered, "Embrace your strength and you will fulfill your destiny. Do not let other people define you."

The boy's eyes went wide. The river talked. He bowed to the river and placed his sword over his heart. "I promise," he said.

The boy began a new way of life. Fresh Roaring Waters had also connected the people to their old ways and infused their culture with spirit, meaning, and the fruits of the sea. It helped the boy begin a new way of life, and even though he met with triumph, many others also needed the river's healing powers.

Throughout the centuries, the river had created inlets, bays, and coves that reshaped the land of the fishermen and the villages in which they lived, changing much of the land's topography. The fishermen still followed the same routes as their ancestors, but luck seemed to have run out for many of them. Day after day they came home without the trout that had fed their families for generations.

One day, a fisherman decided to travel a different route. He got up very early in the morning, much earlier than any of the other fishermen, because he wanted the freedom to explore under the cover of night. He let the moon dictate where his new fishing hole would be. He trusted the moon more than the sun, because the sun seemed to play tricks with the fishermen when they went out after dawn. Mirages caused them to see what they thought were perfect fishing spots. But instead of fish, they discovered rocks that punctured the hulls of their boats. The lone fisherman knew he had to trust something other than the sun and the old routes, or the village would go hungry and many would have to look for another place to live.

The moonlight led the lone fisherman to a special spot along Fresh Roaring Waters that was as smooth as glass, and it provided a great place for him to set anchor and cast his line into the rushing foam where the fish were the most abundant. He watched his line and waited. Nothing happened for a very long time. He didn't get the first nibble on his line until the crack of dawn.

He grabbed his very large net and reached over the bow of his boat, fighting to keep the fish on the line as he reeled in his catch. He swept the net under the fish and plopped it into his boat. There, between the light of the moonset and the sunrise, he gazed at the first fish he'd caught in weeks. It was more beautiful than anything he'd ever seen before.

That one big fish alone would feed his whole family. He put more worms on the end of his line and cast it into the river. This time he got a bite right away, and again he held onto his rod and scooped the fish out of the water with the net. This one was even bigger than the one before. He spent hours filling his boat with fish until it almost sunk under the weight of the trout.

Just after sunset, he set sail for his village. As he headed for the dock, he sailed by other fishermen who were sailing the usual route.

"Where did you find so many fish?" a fisherman asked.

"Did you save any for us?" another inquired.

"They are for the entire village. I found a new spot," the fisherman said.

"New?"

The fishermen stopped their boats. They made a circle around the fisherman whose boat was about to sink under the weight of the trout. They split the catch among all of them, and for the first time in a long time the people of the village went to bed without hunger or worry.

However, worry wasn't far away. Downstream the last person sought the wisdom of the river. Not far from the spot where the fisherman ventured to a new fishing hole in the moonlight, a widow sat at a bench made out of wood so old that it had turned to rock. The lady's boys had grown and the life she'd built around their care, full of education and archery tournaments, had come to a grinding halt. Her life was filled with a silence she never experienced before. It was too silent. She didn't like it when the world went quiet because that left her with her own thoughts, and lately they had been very dark, drowning out the joy of her favorite pastimes like gardening and baking pies. She hadn't baked a pie in a very long, long, time.

She made a habit of coming to the bench because the river kept her company and broke the silence. She enjoyed Fresh Roaring Waters' roars and ripples, and she even thought she had heard it laugh one day. The thought of its laughter kept her coming back.

As she sat there that day, the river delivered a boy with a sword traveling in his boat to the shore where she sat.

"Hello," the widow said.

The boy hadn't seen her yet, so he jumped a little when she spoke.

"Don't be afraid," the widow said.

"Why do you think I'm afraid?" the boy asked.

"Mothers know these things," the widow said.

"Do you have a son?"

"Yes, three, but they are grown now."

"How did you teach them to become strong?" the boy asked.

The widow shuffled in her seat as the glint of the jewels on the boy's sword caught her eye.

"Surely with a sword like that you are already very strong," she said.

He tried to pick up the sword and wield it, but he could only drag it on the ground, as his body was now aching.

"My sons learned how to fall. That's how they learned how to become strong," the widow said.

The boy stopped trying to pick up the sword.

"One day, you will pick it up. Keep trying and don't worry about how long it takes. It takes time to grow into our swords," the woman said.

The boy smiled. He learned not to judge himself for what he didn't know how to do and instead appreciated becoming.

A smile also brightened the widow's face, and she also became filled with the peace of becoming.

The boy waved to the widow before climbing back into his boat. And the widow went home to bake her favorite marionberry pie, no longer bothered by the silence.

GROWTH

IT'S SOFT

It's a nudge
It's a soft nudge
Like the other day in the desert
When I was asking you to show me a sign that you
were near
And in the most silent nothingness of the desert
You appeared in the form of a soft touch on my
sleeve
And the nothingness continued
And I knew then
That you were there
You and I again,
In the midst of that holy land
A holy touch
A holy reunion
In the midst of that holy land.

January 14, 2020
Joshua Tree National Park, California desert

THE WOMAN WHO LISTENED TO ALL MUSIC

nce upon a time, in a mysterious, undiscovered part of the world, there lived a sage woman who had gained all her wisdom by listening to a variety of music. She lived in the now-famous enclave called Tune and Harmony, but things were far from harmonious for her as a young woman.

In those days, she sought refuge from her tumultuous life by traveling the world extensively. She enjoyed learning as much as she could from all of her experiences, from diving deep into sunken cities in azure seas to discovering how her voice carried on the wind as she sang in the mountains. As she traveled, she whittled away at a piece of beautiful wood she had unearthed in the shifting sand dunes of an endless enclave. She whittled every night until the piece of wood wasn't a piece of wood anymore. It had turned into a wonderful instrument.

At first, the whittled instrument sat in her lap. She didn't know where the impulse came from, but she picked it up and placed it on her lips. She trembled a bit before she blew into the mouthpiece, using her fingers to slide its golden rings up, down, and around. The first note came as a surprise and made her heart pound and her palms sweat. The note pleased her, but she blew yet again. This time, the most harmonious music she'd ever heard came out of her instrument and floated on the breeze. Naeltim, the sylph of the air, gently blew the music along, and it traveled in the air over hill-and-dale to the castle of a king and queen in a far-off land on the other side of the world. The music left the king and queen in a quandary. They heard the most beautiful notes in the world but did not know their source. They realized that they had to find the musician at all costs, so they spared no expense to find him.

The woman played the instrument as she traveled across great seas, over mountains, remote deserts, and vast canyons. Music helped her feel calm in the world, especially because much of it didn't make much sense to her. She enjoyed everyone she met, but there were many situations she didn't understand. For not everything she saw was beautiful like the deserts, mountains, canyons, and seas, and her heart broke easily. She played her music to keep her heart whole and happy. It comforted her to know that her music would never leave her, and because of this she never felt alone.

Carrying on with confidence, she opened her mind to everything that came her way on her journey, wanting to soak in what the universe offered. For years, she became a traveling artist and played her beautiful instrument in town squares and villages. Her instrument made a unique melodious sound that left crowds of people mesmerized each time she played.

She dedicated her life to traveling the world because she wanted everyone to receive the peace her music gave, and soon everyone wanted to hear the beautiful sounds that came from the instrument she had created.

"How can we ever repay you for the peace we feel?" a villager asked.

"Your smile alone is sufficient," she said.

"No, we insist. Please have this donkey, or this horse. Surely it would make your way easier then traveling on foot?"

"No, thank you. I enjoy traveling slowly. If I ride on a donkey or a horse I might miss something," she said.

"There must be something. Our village was so grim before you arrived and played your music for us. Tell us what we can do!" another villager begged.

"I will take a payment in music. Just one song is all I require in return. Please play me whatever music you love," the young woman said. And this practice helped her expand her repertoire, and her music never grew old.

Kings and queens around the world loved her music so much that they paid for her travels so they could hear the otherworldly sound of her instrument. She wanted to walk, but they insisted she travel by royal carriage because they couldn't wait to hear her music. Not even the sweetest songbird could have sung such incredible melodies.

One day, a little boy came up to her after she played one of her concerts and asked, "How can you make such beautiful music? What is your instrument called?"

And the woman, who had heard the same question a million of times before, always gave the same response. "My music is a combination of all the music I have listened to throughout my travels, and my instrument has no name."

But this time, the little boy, who just like all little boys and girls, was more insightful than the grown-ups, replied, "Your music makes me happy, but it also makes me sad. Why is that?"

The woman had a secret she infused into her music. She knew that if she wove her secret within the notes, then her listeners would feel the pull of both the happiness and the sadness in the songs.

She smiled and said, "My music makes you happy and sad because it is a blend of all the music I have listened to from around the world. Everywhere I go, I listen to music, and I add those notes into my musical chords. My music also makes you sad because you have fallen in love with the questions of your heart."

"My heart asks questions?" the boy said.

"Yes, of course it does," the young woman said.

"What is the greatest question a heart can ask?" the boy said.

"Many people have forgotten how to be happy. They struggle with knowing what is enough. So, I try to take their heart's question and fold it into my music. Sadness isn't something to run away from. It's just a note on a scale. And to make wonderful music, we need to play all of our notes."

"But I don't like those notes. They are hard to listen to," the boy said.

"My music is the music of the world. And that's also why it also makes you feel things you have never felt before. I blend what I see, hear, feel, taste, and smell into an orchestral ballet," she said, holding up her funny-looking instrument.

"But don't you become sad when you create sad music?"

"Not at all! I love ALL music because it speaks to me. Music is powerful because it teaches that it's okay to be sad, just as much as it is okay to be happy. That it's important to love all of who we are and accept all the emotions we hold. My audiences enjoy listening to my music because when they stay open to listening to unfamiliar and familiar notes, even those that evoke intense emotions, they open up to listening to all of their feelings. Our feelings are important, because they teach us where to go and what to do! Great music makes us feel like we are taking a journey of the heart."

The boy treasured the wisdom the woman imparted that day. And she did the same with many children around the world. Then one day, the woman had too many invitations to accept them all. Since she couldn't be everywhere, and was needed everywhere at once, she didn't know what to do. So she enlisted an archer she had met on her journey to shoot his arrows at a target to determine where she should play her music next.

Unbeknownst to the woman, something had gone terribly wrong. Her music wasn't just enjoyed for the wisdom and knowledge it imparted, but had become an addiction. The people who had recently heard her music made requests to have her play again, again, and again. Some people followed her caravan on the road just so they would know where she would be playing next. And so the woman needed men on horseback to protect her carriage, and she also needed a band of men in shining armor to escort her safely on stage. And she once again sought comfort in her music. She never knew that she could feel so all alone in huge crowds of shouting, adoring fans, even as all her dreams seemed to have come true.

At the end of one of her concerts, she clutched her instrument and vowed that she would give up music forever. She wanted to end the darkness in her heart and the pain of never really connecting with people because it was deemed too dangerous for her to meet the crowds after her performance.

Backstage, to the deafening sound of applause, she put the instrument down for the last time.

At that moment, the king and queen who had spared no expense to learn the identity of the most incredible musician they had ever heard, approached the outdoor theatre where she played. Like breadcrumbs, the music had led them straight to her. They sent Sir Makelvee to engage with the knights of the woman.

"I am sorry, but she plays no more," the woman's knight replied.

"But there must be some mistake?" Sir Makelvee said. "The King and Queen of Venerova are here and wish her to become part of their royal court."

When the woman heard this, she came out of the shadows.

"A royal court?" the woman asked.

Sir Makelvee turned to the woman and bowed down. "Yes, my lady."

"We will provide you a safe haven to inspire the world with your music," the king said.

Everyone in the area bowed to the king.

"You may rise," the king nodded to all assembled there.

"It is important to protect something so precious. We will give you a beautiful, safe kingdom where you can wander the hills and explore your music without fear," the king said. "And most importantly, your music will never stop."

The Woman Who Listened to All Music lived out her days in peace, exploring her music in the kingdom of Tune and Harmony, where people could gather outside the moat and lay their picnic blankets, and enjoy their delicacies as she gave her concerts from behind the palace walls. And she named her instrument Acceptance.

EMBRACE

THE TREE
OF LIFE

It is no coincidence
That I find myself here
Healing myself
In Joshua Tree
Wearing my tree of life ring
Waiting to plant those twenty-one trees for you.
They are all gentle reminders
That are always in front of me when I need them
In these very different forms
Of colors, sights, and people
Even a picture hanging on the wall
Depicting the Tree of Life
Suddenly reminds me again that it all continues
And that Love creates life,
And because Love cannot die,
Life does not die, but transforms.
With infinite gratitude
I see that Life remodels in all of its formations,
shapes and designs
And the colors and sights and people
Will then appear completely different
And all will be soft and gentle

But the nudges and the signs will not always be so
immediately evident
Because I have been so used to the current form.
They will be soft and gentle,
As soft and gentle is the understanding
That I am loved
No matter what
Because Love is soft
Love is gentle
And once I ask from my heart
I know that I will be heard
And in time, I will always be helped
Because that has been the story
Of the Tree of my Life.

January 17, 2020
Twentynine Palms, California desert

NIAMI AND THE TREE OF LIFE

nce upon a time, Naeltim, the sylph of the air, blew a wind of change that transported Niami to the middle of the Mojave Desert. The soft wind picked her up and placed her in front of the Tree of Life, a Joshua tree.

Niami didn't know what to think of this sudden change. One minute she was crying in her bedroom in the city, mourning the loss of her mother, and the next she was hot, weary, and alone. She was a stranger in a strange land, in front of the strangest tree she'd ever seen. The Joshua tree didn't look like a tree at all, but more like a bush on steroids.

But the Tree of Life captured Niami's imagination. Its bunches of spindly leaves made the tree look like it had a head and two hands outstretched toward the sky. The woman believed that the tree was praying because of the way the limbs looked to her. Niami didn't want to disturb the tree, but the sight of its head and outstretched branches brought her an overwhelming feeling of tranquility. Since she'd never felt that kind of peace before, she thought she'd find out if the Tree of Life could help her. She'd often heard tales of the Tree of Life and now that she was face-to-face with its strange beauty, she became brave enough to speak her truth.

"Tree of Life, I'm tired of seeing things being born and needlessly dying. I wonder why I cannot also be a Tree of Life too. I don't want to be human anymore. Can I join you? Can you turn me into a wise tree and teach me all that you know?"

It took some time for Niami to hear the Tree of Life's reply because the hot desert wind howled, and she couldn't make out its voice very well. For at first, it spoke in almost a whisper. She expected its voice to be booming. She tried to harder and harder to listen as the wind blew louder and louder. Oh, how she wished the Tree of Life would speak up and speak faster. For she didn't want to miss a word, and she wanted to know all the answers to her questions as soon as possible. She hated waiting. She didn't want to feel pain inside her heart anymore and longed to gain as much wisdom from the tree as she possibly could.

"You, Niami, are a unique expression of the universe," the Tree of Life said, rather dismissively, Naimi thought. "You don't need to be anything or anyone else."

"But I'm tired of being me. I'm tired of the pain from losing those I love. I'm tired of having to begin again every time hardship comes to my doorstep, of being strong," Niami said.

"My dear, if you only experienced joy you would never value it. For without sorrow, you and I would never have met. You would never have come to visit me. You would never grow in the way the universe needs you to grow," the Tree of Life said.

"Are you a lonely tree? Is that why you pray?" the woman asked.

"There's a difference between being lonely and being alone, my dear," the Tree of Life replied.

"But you are so beautiful and so happy here in your wild solitude. I want to be more like you," Niami said. "For I am neither happy nor beautiful."

"Happiness is a choice, my dear Niami," the Tree of Life said.

Niami didn't know what to say to that. *Is it that easy? Can I just choose to be happy?*

"Be proud of all that you are. If we were all the same form, made-up of the same thoughts, only experiencing times of joy and no times of trial, we wouldn't be the expression the universe needs us to be. We would simply exist, and beauty, joy, and hope wouldn't find a firm foundation in our lives," the Tree of Life said.

"How can I be more like you? Everything in me changes constantly, and I'm fed up with this chaos in my heart. I'm never able to be peaceful and still," the woman said. It was then that the wind stopped blowing so hard, and a silence fell over the Mojave, the kind of silence that lets us see deeply into who we are and our experience in the world. And then it hit her—she hadn't asked the most important question of all.

"Why are you called the Tree of Life?"

The silence of the great desert washed over Niami.

"My dear, I will tell you but first I want you to know that I am happy and I am at peace because you gave birth to me. I would not be alive if it weren't for you!"

Niami didn't understand how the Tree of Life, something so sacred and ancient, owed its existence to her, a woman of seemingly little value to many people in her life. She took two steps closer to the tree, just to be sure she had heard it right.

"You need me?"

"Yes. I'm called the Tree of Life because I give life to lots of creatures who wouldn't survive without me. You see, if it weren't for the yucca moth, I wouldn't be alive. I also wouldn't be alive without you, because I need your questions to grow."

"You need me?"

"Do you see the way my branches twist and turn?"

Niami's eyes went wide, because she hadn't really noticed before. "Yes, I do."

"They are reminders, my sweet child, to keep your soul strong by turning toward your future. Always turning toward your future. Do not be a creature of the past."

Niami followed the twists and turns of one of the tree's branches as she listened.

"It's why the sylph of the air blew you here," the Tree of Life said.

"Is that what happened?" Niami asked.

"Yes, it is." the Tree of Life replied.

"Why does the sylph do that? I've never heard of the sylph of the air."

"He blew you here so that you would learn that individuality lies in the soul, and it is always in a process of becoming. It's a delicate dance between acknowledging and learning from the past, as you turn from it into the great thrill of what is to come and all that you will be. Embrace this time of change, my dear. May I tell you why?"

"Please!" Niami was growing more enchanted with the Tree of Life's every word.

"I will share with you one of my secrets. Most flowers come and go, their beauty is here today and gone tomorrow. Yet my flowers change the direction of my growth. They are both beautiful and a sign of a new direction. Once flowers appear on one of my branches, it can no longer continue growing."

"I didn't know that flowers, something so little and so beautiful, can cause that much change," Niami said.

"It is similar to you, my dear. You will find that when you bloom, there will be a subtle change in your growth. Enjoy the new direction and do not lament at the cost."

"I love that flowers are so powerful!" Niami said. One of her favorite things to do in the whole wide world was to skip through the forest and make bouquets of the wildflowers that bloomed there in the springtime.

"Ah, but what's more important still is the foundation that we lay. The how of what we do."

"The how?" Niami took a closer look at the Tree of Life's flowers.

"See, for the first few decades of my life I didn't flower."

"What? How can that be? How come it took so long? Weren't you sad?" Niami said.

"I had to hold back for a long time to become strong enough to support my full, white, luscious flowers, which beautifully reflect the moonlight on dark desert nights when their sweet fragrance is most potent. When the yucca moths come around to pollinate my flowers, I provide them a place to take care of their young and I am key to their survival. And so you can see how my fellow trees all grow very differently, in ways that are unexpected and unique."

Niami looked all around the desert at every other tree. They were all different but yet the same.

"Like you, we are what our blooms make us."

"I guess I understand. I am you and you are me," Niami said.

INTERCONNECTION

STOP, LISTEN
AND HEAL

Taking a break from everything and everyone
Talking to my own spirit
And taking my time to heal.
I am in the desert because it cleanses me
And I can hear everything now
Away from all the noises and distractions,
The beautiful mornings in the desert
Teach me the gift of peace again after the turmoil
And the silence, and the lights twinkling far away
Are just as sweet and tender
As your beautiful soul
Shimmering gently in my heart.

January 17, 2020
Twentynine Palms, California desert

SPRINGY BUNNY AND THE PURPLE FAIRY GODMOTHER

pringy Bunny was a happy, always-excited-to-do-something-outside-in-the-sunshine bunny who lived in Cottontail Valley of the Moon. But she hated Cottontail Valley of the Moon during winter, when its aspen trees were covered in snow and the ground was very cold. Some days she couldn't go outside. She didn't like being confined in the little house where she lived with her mama, daddy, and fifty-seven other bunny siblings.

In winter, she was only allowed outside the family burrow on the rare days that the cold wind didn't blow. During moments like these, she happily hopped around the forest, foraging for acorn treasures hidden underneath the snow. She loved to gather them up and bring them to her mother, who made Springy's favorite carrot-acorn stew.

But the aspen trees made foraging difficult. One morning, a light breeze blew an aspen branch back and forth, resulting in a blizzard of snow. A million snowflakes fell down on Springy Bunny, freezing her whiskers. The next minute, mounds of snow plopped down on top of her, nearly burying her alive. She almost got plopped to death when the large snowball fell from the tree branch high above her, just as she went to pick up the last acorn.

Suddenly stuck in a snow mound, Springy used her powerful hind legs to punch her way out. She grabbed her charming little wicker basket and hopped all the way back home. Breathless, she opened the heavy wooden door to her burrow and ran right into Mama, with her eyes as big as saucers.

"Whatever is the matter, Springy?" Mama said, in that calm way that all mamas have when danger lurks all around.

"I almost got killed by the snow that fell from the branch of the aspen tree!" Springy Bunny said in between gasps of air to catch her breath.

"Well, why ever were you out there little Springy?" Mama asked, covering Springy with a homemade afghan. Mama had made fifty-seven of them, one for each of her children. They all had their names woven into the yarn so each bunny would never fight over their blankets. Springy snuggled up in her afghan, feeling much calmer and warmer.

"Here! I gathered more acorns for the stew!" Springy Bunny said, pulling her almost-full basket of acorns out from under the afghan. She offered the basket to Mama, who grabbed it gingerly.

"Why thank you, Springy!" Mama Bunny said with a smile.

She set Springy's basket down on the kitchen counter and carefully removed the acorns from the basket and put them into the stew. She gave the pot a few long, careful stirs.

"I have just enough now," Mama Bunny said, giving her little bunny a hug.

Springy leaned her head into Mama's soft fur and breathed in the scent of the acorn stew bubbling on the stove. It made the whole burrow smell fabulous. If Springy ever made perfume, she would find a way to put Mama's stew scent in a bottle and call the fragrance "Home."

"Now gather around, all you cute little bunnies, it's story time," Mama said. She loved telling stories to pass the time, especially during the cold winters.

Soon the scurrying of her fifty-seven bunny babies filled the burrow. When they were all sitting attentively and all their eyes were on her, Mama picked up her storybook. She sat in the same little wooden rocking chair she always sat in at story time, beside the metal stove. Springy Bunny sat at Mama's feet, curled up in her afghan like all the rest of her bunny brothers and sisters.

"Cottontail Valley of the Moon had always been a valley filled with sunshine, vivid flowers, and colorful trees where bunnies and their babies lived freely," Mama began.

"They loved playing hopping games, and they ate bright orange carrots and sometimes even the most colorful peppers. Life was always joyful in Cottontail Valley of the Moon, where the sun always shone and love and laughter filled the valley up to the mountain tops, all year long."

"When will it be like that again, Mama?" Springy Bunny asked. She was a naive, innocent, milk-drinking baby bunny with fluffy legs and long, furry ears.

"When the Purple Fairy Godmother visits and makes everything right again," Mama Bunny said. Then she continued, "One day a strong wind blew through Cottontail Valley of the Moon. It was so strong and sudden that it caught all the bunnies by surprise and sent them chaotically hopping back to their homes. They waited for this strange thing called 'cold air' to pass. But the cold wind didn't go away. It blew and blew for many days. It was so strong that it destroyed all the colorful flowers, overturned many of the colorful trees, and blew all the bright orange carrots and even the most colorful peppers away.

"All the rabbits and bunnies of Cottontail Valley of the Moon trembled and frantically stared out of their windows as the clouds blew into their precious valley and covered the sun. All the colorful things they loved disappeared in no time at all. Then, the clouds darkened and carpeted the valley in a deep layer of snow. They learned to live in this cold world, but it was very, very hard on the little bunnies and their families. This new cold season visited them every year, and they called it winter. They all dreamed of the day that the Purple Fairy Godmother would come and set everything right. And so they waited for the jolly fairy with ginger-colored hair and a glowing purple dress to fly down from her fairy wonderland, golden magic wand in hand, to undo the terrible curse. They looked forward to the day when the fairy would restore their beautiful valley to a colorful time without winter."

Soon all the baby bunnies fell fast asleep. All except Springy Bunny, "Now off to sleep with you, my little darling," Mama said, patting Springy on the head. "We'll have more of the story tonight."

Springy Bunny laid down to try and take a long afternoon nap next to her bunny brothers and sisters. She longed for the perpetual summer of the past, when she was free to go outside and hop around happily and play as much as she wanted, running free with the thousands of her friends who also lived in Cottontail Valley of the Moon.

Springy Bunny was the sort of bunny that no one could stop. She always wanted to play and always wanted to be around her bunny friends. She loved to play hide-and-seek around Cottontail Valley of the Moon, smell the colorful flowers, and eat as many orange, juicy carrots as she could. One day, she even had a carrot-eating contest with her best bunny friends and won first place! That was the sort of bunny that Springy Bunny was.

But it was a particularly cold and snowy winter in Cottontail Valley of the Moon, and carrots were scarce. Springy Bunny couldn't stop thinking about eating carrots. Instead of sleeping, Springy Bunny walked over to the tiny window in her tiny house and stared out on the icy landscape. Flurries were covering Cottontail Valley of the Moon with snow, and she could no longer see her favorite bunny trails. Restless and sad, Springy realized she wouldn't be able to go outside and play hide-and-seek or participate in fun carrot-eating contests for a very long time. While she could still do lots of things at home, like play Carrot Counting and Carrot Toss, or listen to Mama's stories by the fire, she still couldn't hop down her favorite trails when she wanted.

She didn't like to slow down. And just at the moment when she decided she'd never slow down ever again, Springy Bunny saw something in the distance outside the frosty window of her warm, little home—a jolly fairy with ginger-colored hair and a glowing purple dress, flying around with her gold magic wand.

Springy rubbed her eyes in disbelief, as the Purple Fairy Godmother came closer to the window and smiled at Springy Bunny.

With the brightness of five thousand seven hundred little glow bugs, the Purple Fairy Godmother looked at Springy Bunny and said in hushed tones, "I love you, and I want to teach you that winter will soon pass and that slowing down now is important."

Springy Bunny quickly wiped the frosted window, and replied, "Purple Fairy, I feel lost and I want to go and play outside."

Mama and Daddy, after hearing the voices, came to Springy Bunny's side and gazed out the window. They were so pleased they were to be granted a meeting with the Purple Fairy Godmother that they asked her to come inside.

"Would you like a cup of warm milk to share by the fire?"

"I would be delighted!" the Purple Fairy Godmother said with a big smile, in her happy-go-lucky tone.

After sitting by the fire and drinking her cup of warm milk, the Purple Fairy Godmother returned their kindness by sharing a story with the entire family.

"Once upon a time, there was a hoppy, happy, and jolly white bunny named Whippy who did not listen to Mama and Daddy and left the house during wintertime. The mommies and the daddies would not allow their babies to go out and play because freezing temperatures would have hurt them. Because they loved their bunny babies very much, they kept their children inside their little homes and warm by the fire, waiting for winter to end.

"Whippy Bunny decided to pack her little bag with as many carrots as she could and leave the house to go see her friend Cheery Bunny. But while she was out in the forest, she decided to take a shortcut to her friend's house through a different part of Cottontail Valley of the Moon. It wasn't long before Whippy Bunny got lost. She looked around, but all she could see were the trees aching under the weight of so much snow. Nervously, Whippy reached into her bag for a carrot, but because she'd hopped so fast, every carrot had fallen out of her bag. So now, she was not only cold, but very hungry too.

"All of a sudden, Whippy heard a very peculiar noise in the midst of the snowy woods. She couldn't pinpoint where the noise actually was coming from, but it definitely sounded like rustling. Almost like something moving between the trees. But whatever it was had moved so fast and so unexpectedly that when she turned around, she saw nothing. Nothing except really, really HUGE footprints, and so DEEP that she, a tiny, milk-drinking and carrot-eating bunny, would never have imagined that so big of a creature existed.

"'It's just my imagination,' Whippy said.

"Hungry for carrots, she kept moving along nervously when all of a sudden, there it was again. The same rustling. This time, Whippy figured out where it was coming from. Whatever it was was lurking behind one of the snowy aspen trees.

"Whippy couldn't move. Tiny little balls of ice had formed underneath her tiny little paws, and she shivered in terror. She'd thought that she would reach Cheery Bunny's house very quickly, but she hadn't considered that the deep snow would make it so difficult to hop all the way to Cheery's house. She hadn't counted on the rustling and huge, deep footprints in the snow either.

"All of a sudden, Whippy heard another noise. This one was REALLY scary, like a whistle that turned into a growl. Slowly, she lifted her eyes to face the frightening sound. An enormous aspen tree shook in front of her. It was the scariest moment in

Whippy Bunny's life. Her tiny little white paws were frozen to the ground, and she only had enough strength left to tremble at the sight of what stood before her. Whippy Bunny's frozen paws and terrible fear forced her to stop. She noticed a white, furry hand grabbing the trunk of the tree. Only then could she hear her little heart pounding.

"The Wamble was forced to stop too. He hid behind the tree when he heard the bunny hopping. The fifty-seven-foot tall Abominable Snowman of Cottontail Valley of the Moon had the best hearing of any animal on Earth, but he seldom chose to pay attention. From behind the safety of the tree, he tried to come to terms with his fear.

"Wamble was just as scared of Whippy as Whippy was scared of Wamble.

"Try and say that three times fast," the Purple Fairy Godmother said to the fifty-seven children staring at her with big, worried bunny eyes.

The burrow buzzed with the bunnies, taking the Purple Fairy Godmother up on her challenge.

"Okay, okay! Hush!" Mama Bunny said.

The buzzing subsided.

"Let the Purple Fairy Godmother finish!" Daddy Bunny said. He was way more into the story than Springy Bunny ever thought he'd ever be since he wasn't the one who told the stories at story time.

"The Wamble was not your normal abominable snowman," the Purple Fairy Godmother continued. "Even though he might have looked like just any other abominable snowman with long white fur and monstrous fangs, he was a very shy snowman who lived by himself. The only abominable snowman in Cottontail Valley of the Moon had bunny phobia. Every time he saw one, he hid behind a tree and trembled in terror. He didn't shake the tree on purpose. He was so enormous that when he shivered in fear, he'd shake up an entire aspen tree. And sometimes it made small blizzards appear out of nowhere, or made plops of snow nearly bury bunnies alive while they foraged.

"The Wamble lived in Cottontail Valley of the Moon only during the winter season, and he had one very specific duty. The Counsel of the Master Rabbits of Cottontail Valley of the Moon had appointed the Wamble to frighten all the tiny bunnies who didn't listen to their mommies and daddies and left their homes without asking for permission. The Wamble was supposed to scare the bunnies who didn't stop and listen to their parents so that they would hop back home to safety, and not leave their tiny homes until winter was over."

Springy Bunny thought about the light breeze that had blown an aspen branch and the blizzard of snow that had dropped a million snowflakes down and frozen her whiskers. She thought about how the mounds of snow had plopped down on top of her, nearly burying her alive.

"The Wamble?" Springy Bunny whispered.

"You see, many years before, the Counsel of the Master Rabbits of Cottontail Valley of the Moon decided to congregate and brainstorm a solution to the dilemma of the big wind that sent a chill into their little bit of paradise every winter. They just could not understand what had happened and why," the Purple Fairy Godmother continued.

"So, they sent an ambassador to Winterside Valley, a valley that was the exact opposite of what Cottontail Valley usually was: a perpetual, colorful summer. Instead, it was a cold, damp, dark, and very sad place. Winter ruled year-round in Winterside Valley, where Hermia the Enchantress was the Queen of the Abominable Snowmen. She was jealous of all the happiness and laughter that reigned in Cottontail Valley of the Moon. The bunnies' happiness fueled her anger. And so one day, the Enchantress decided to use her strongest winds to destroy as much of the color and joy and warmth as she could.

"She only stopped when every single colorful thing in Cottontail Valley had been destroyed. So when the Master Rabbits of Cottontail Valley of the Moon came to her to ask for help, she offered them a proposal: 'I will offer you all the green spinach from Winterside Valley every winter . . .'

The Master Rabbits collectively gasped, for spinach is a delicacy among bunnies in Cottontail Valley of the Moon, and they hadn't eaten any in what seemed like a lifetime.

"'. . . but you will have to have one cold, wet and snowy winter every year. We will take that warmth and have a summer for the first time in our lives. If you do not accept, I will keep destroying your land until you will have nothing of summer ever again!'

"The Master Council of Rabbits agreed with one caveat. They wanted Winterside Valley to allow one of their vast number of abominable snowmen to act as the official frightener of runaway bunnies. The Enchantress assigned Wamble from Winterside Valley to the job precisely because of his bunny phobia. She was not only a jealous enchantress but also very cruel."

"But what about Cheery Bunny?" Springy said.

"Cheery Bunny had been waiting for her friend Whippy all day long, and because it had started to become dark, she began to feel very nervous. She kept going to the frosty window of the tiny house that she shared with her Mama and Daddy and her siblings, searching for a glimpse of her little friend, but all she could see was a blizzard. Hours and hours went by, and Cheery had a lump in her throat because all she wanted to do was cry. Cheery's Mama said to her, 'What is the matter, my baby?'

'Mama, I have something to tell you,' she said.

'Oh?' Mama said with a wrinkled brow.

'I've been waiting for Whippy Bunny all day. Polly the Woodpecker has been communicating between us and arranged our meeting. I have been waiting and waiting, but I'm now worried.'

"That's when Cheery Bunny and her mama and dad left the tiny house and started looking for Whippy Bunny. But you see, Whippy's mama and dad had left their tiny house and had started looking for their daughter at the exact same time.

"Desperate to find the little milk-drinking and carrot-eating bunny, they all ventured into the high snow, following the path that led to each other's tiny houses. Because they all left at the same time, they met half-way, where to their dismay, they heard an uncontrollable, loud sobbing coming from behind one of the aspen trees.

"The sight was unimaginable—a fifty-seven-foot Abominable Snowman cried while gently holding tiny Whippy Bunny in his enormous furry hands. Whippy had frozen, and the Wamble thought that she'd died.

"As you know, the Wamble's hearing was very acute, and although the two mamas and papas had tried to be as cautious and quiet as possible while approaching him, he immediately heard the muffled noises. In a great fright, he dropped Whippy Bunny back in the snow, and ran away. No one ever saw the Wamble again.

"Whippy Bunny awoke immediately after being dropped in the deep snow. She cried in terror. Both mamas and papas ran to her. Whippy's mama picked her up, hugging her as snugly as she could.

"'Shhh . . . stop crying, Whippy,' Mama said. 'Listen to me now. I'm here. Shhh . . . I'm here. We are here. It's time for you to melt all this frost on your tiny paws and go back home. You will be safe there, and you will be warm. We have a nice mug of warm milk waiting for you.'

"Whippy cried again, this time with joy and relief as Naeltim, the sylph of the air, blew a soft warm wind in Whippy Bunny's frozen fur, melting away all the ice out of her tender pink paws. She could finally move again.

"And that is how perpetual summer came back to Cottontail Valley of the Moon. The enchantress lost her powers when Naeltim, the sylph of the air, chased the winter away. And the little bunnies in the valley never had to worry about Wambles and Wambles never had to worry about bunnies ever again."

HEAL

THE NOISE
IS GONE

How I can now clearly see
That it's just a thick illusion,
This wall between you and I:
It is a temporary stay.
And you and I have never ceased
Just briefly separated by things
And stuff
That in the end are helping us
Understand.

January 17, 2020
Twentynine Palms, California desert

THE SONG
OF TWO WINDS

wo lovely, very different winds known as the trade winds played together, at the end of one of the largest rainbows the Earth has ever seen. The rainbow stretched from one side of the Earth all the way to the other side. It was so big that it arched over the northern and southern hemispheres, spanning cities, oceans, lakes, mountains, canyons, hidden towns, and secluded streets in such a way that every person on Earth could see the rainbow at the same time.

The two winds didn't know it, but as they played, they created a rare beauty that brought people out of their everyday lives and into lives of enchantment and awe. Those are two of the most important things on Earth, for when we discover the power of wonder and joy, anything is possible.

Perhaps you have encountered the winds at play. Have you ever taken a silent walk in the woods and heard the whoosh of the wind in the treetops? Or been on a mountaintop and heard the rush of the wind through the canyons below? You were on the winds' playground at the perfect time, for you heard their playfulness and witnessed something that made you stop and perhaps close your eyes. Or maybe you said things like, "Did you hear that?" You sensed them in the air. Nothing makes the winds happier than when those of the Earth notice them at play.

They loved chasing each other through all the beautiful and hidden places of the world, even into the deepest darkest caves. They had fun following the leader and running after each other. All the while, they sang their winding, windy songs and danced to the tune of the Earth as they rushed by trees, rock formations and gorges, around the sharpest corners of the world's tallest buildings, through long tunnels, and even along the sleek bodies of jet planes. Each song was a little different, as varied as their playful natures and the joys they brought to the people of the Earth.

The winds created things like storms, which nourished the land, made rivers flow stronger and wider, and brought life to the desert. They loved blowing away treacherous tempests to let the land bask in sunshine, helping crops grow, children play, and ships sail on fair seas.

Because they played, they also brought about the winds of change. As lightning departed and the savage seas calmed, sailors navigated their way across impossibly vast oceans, children climbed higher on monkey bars as the sun dried up soggy playgrounds, and the desert bloomed. The winds liked to bring about changes that surprised the humans of the Earth, who would not learn the joy of playing until their spirits learned to dance to the tune of the heavens.

The universe named one of those winds Naeltim, the sylph of the air, a soft, warm wind from the south. Although his wind was soft, his was the wind of positive transformation. His best friend, the Wind of the North, had no name. Unlike Naeltim, she took on unique personalities depending on the origin of her gusts. Used to colder temperatures, the Wind of the North adapted to the places that she found herself in and never saw the need to settle on one name. Hers was the wind of adaptation.

Since the winds were best friends, they hated parting. But they knew that the world needed them desperately, and sometimes in service to those of the Earth, they had to separate. One would fly to the north and the other would fly to the south, bringing the winds of transformation and adaptation to where those of the Earth needed them most. At times, they rushed their work to make their separation shorter, causing unintended side effects like tornadoes, hurricanes, and firenadoes. So they learned to take their time. They understood that it was best for the Earth and for each other when the universe called on them to separate. So, they accepted that sometimes distance healed the invisible parts of themselves, which was the best thing for the winds and the Earth.

Because they were best friends, they couldn't stand being apart, but they knew that without their help, Earth would fall into terrible trouble with famines, floods, and all kinds of things that one cannot see, like broken dreams and shattered spirits. And, because their duties sometimes took them to the most disparate places around the Earth, they sometimes forgot that they would meet again one day.

One time, the Earth called the winds to part dramatically as they played in the Mediterranean Sea. The Wind of the North needed to bring Arctic snow up to the glaciers on the top of the world so they would continue to provide shelter for the polar bears, caribou, and Arctic foxes. The temperature had risen so quickly that the situation had become desperate.

"I must go now, Naeltim. Many people and animals are in trouble," the Wind of the North said.

"I, too, must go. There is a windstorm settling over the Sahara, and I need to make sure the dust cloud will not choke the people in Africa before it heads over the Atlantic. They need my air," Naeltim said.

Together the Wind of the North and Naeltim, the sylph of the air, played over the Mediterranean one last time. As they danced inside and outside of each other's wakes, they caused a waterspout. People from the shores of Spain and Morocco spotted the sight of the water rising and swirling out of the calm sea, close to the Rock of Gibraltar. Captivated by the waterspout's beauty, people on the banks of the sea wondered why the water rose out of the ocean on such a cloudless day. They knew not that the winds were at play.

So off they went. The Wind of the North whooshed to the Arctic Circle. Naeltim softly drifted over the equator to stem the tide of the Godzilla-like dust cloud in the Sahara. Their duties were varied, as they were crucial to the fate of the Earth.

Naeltim, the sylph of the air, tried but couldn't completely calm the gargantuan cloud over the enormous area of Sahara. Slowly, Naeltim infused the air with more oxygen from Morocco to Algeria, across Egypt and Libya, then down to Sudan and Tunisia. The expansive cloud eventually left on its long, long trip across the Atlantic where, on the other side of the world, it would settle onto the beaches of the Caribbean as sand.

The Wind of the North—because she had spent so much time with her best friend, and because she enjoyed the pace of Mediterranean life—took the same slow but deliberate pace to harvest the intense cold of the world and bring it to the Arctic.

But she couldn't just conjure the temperatures she needed. She had to go deep into the coldest expanses of the world and harness their powers of extreme cold to save the glaciers. The treacherous journey began in Snag, in the Yukon Territory, where the Earth had registered its coldest temperatures ever. She breathed in the record-breaking cold and held it close as she flew. She journeyed to North Ice, Greenland, a land almost covered in ice and snow. Yet again, she took a deep breath, sending a crushing chill into most of her warm places. She held onto the cold as she traveled to Ulaanbaatar, Mongolia and breathed in its permafrost.

The last of the warmth that the Wind of the North held completely disappeared. Only then could she unleash the cold that could reverse the melt of the troubled glacier. It was at this moment that she missed Naeltim the most. When they played, nothing felt too big or too hard or impossible. Together they had discovered the power of playfulness and the importance of fun. The memory of the waterspout by the Rock of Gibraltar gave the Wind of the North the energy to release all the frigid wind she'd collected from the coldest parts of the Earth. And as she blew, the warm glow of her friendship with Naeltim warmed her again, and she could move easily, once again hearing the songs of the wind play on the sharp edges of the icebergs and hollowed-out ice caves.

The ocean froze at the touch of her breath. One by one, icy bridges formed out of the sea from glacier to glacier, ensuring the effortless movement of the wild animals of the Arctic. Once again, life was easy and plentiful. As the Wind of the North got ready to rendezvous with Naeltim, she noticed a family of polar bears playing on the ice, celebrating the birth of their new baby polar bear.

Both exhausted, the Wind of the North and Naeltim met at the Perch, a place of comfort and rest that they always returned to after their important work. Naeltim was the first to arrive, so he made a special surprise for the Wind of the North.

The Wind of the North had a long journey to the Perch. She thought she might not make it. For air is comprised of small bits of water, and hers had all frozen in the tundra of the Arctic. She thought she might break into a million pieces and melt away. But as she traveled over the Himalayas, the scent of gardenias filled the air. The Wind of the North breathed in the gardenia-scented air deeply. Then the scent turned to lilacs, then lavender, and finally, spiced honey.

The scents filled her with joy, for the Arctic had many wonders, but nothing like the scents of the south. Naeltim spotted the Wind of the North cycling down through the canyon, just below the Perch. He chased after his best friend, and together they danced and spun, soared, and plummeted.

The Wind of the North said, "My work was very hard and very cold. I almost gave up."

"What happened?" Naeltim said.

"I felt as if I'd blow apart in the cold and break into a million pieces," the Wind of the North said. "But then I smelled something divine."

"My present to you," Naeltim said. "I flew to a town called Grasse in France, where they make the most exquisite perfumes on Earth. I filled the Perch with the fragrances and hoped the surprise would be something that you, my dear best friend, would remember forever."

Together the trade winds settled into the Perch and watched another rainbow form over the Earth. It had waited for them, just like a child awaits his mother's return.

PLAY

IN THE END

In the end, it doesn't matter what they say
You are me, and I am you.
In the cosmic dance of it all,
I see you in that bird, I see you in the sand,
And you are in the wind.
The vast openness gently reminds me
Of the greatness of it all
And that we are all One
And that we are water, fire, and Love
And that it doesn't matter what they say,
Because I simply know,
That you are me, and I am you.

January 17, 2020
Twentynine Palms, California desert

THE POET AND THE FABULOUS THUNDERBIRD

n uninspired, confused poet looked out of his window. Although he lived in a quaint, storybook village on a vast expanse of rolling hillsides, on this day he found nothing in the beauty of nature to inspire him. This continued day after day for weeks. His sad conundrum had begun when he became disheartened by the realities of the dark world in which he lived.

Famine, pestilence, and drought had plagued the land for many months. Long gone were the fields of green, green grass, and beautiful wildflowers. The village's terrible fate and his own lack of energy and inspiration vexed him so totally that he could no longer dream up anything that he cared to write about. Nothing inspired him anymore. Weeks turned into months where he never picked up his pen.

Before the crisis, he had been an inspiration to all who knew him. Many spoke of the lightness and beauty they sensed in his presence and from reading his words. But lately, he felt heavy, and the heaviness caused his appearance to change. No longer handsome, no longer shining his beauty into the world, the poet was unrecognizable even to those who had been closest to him.

So, his closest friends didn't inquire about how the poet was feeling or what he was working on, because he'd become invisible to them. He felt lost and alone, and the one thing he had always counted on to bring him out of the darkness had left him completely—his poetry.

One day, he decided to take a walk in the forest because nature had always spoken to his soul, the place where great poetry was born. He hoped it would help find the parts of himself that were missing. When the poet came to his favorite lake, he laid down beside it and stretched out on the cool long grass, as he once had on other long afternoons when poems seemed to race from his fingers and onto the page. Everyone in town had words of encouragement and praise for those poems.

That day though, the poet unpacked his pen and paper from his knapsack and set it in front of him. He expected his fingers to race across the page as they always had when he sat there. But his fingers didn't move. They didn't even want to hold the pen.

As a diversion, he leaned over the lake and stared at his reflection. He didn't even recognize himself anymore. His long, smooth golden locks had turned dark and wiry. His once brilliant blue eyes had faded and became washed out, and his red cheeks and lips had become chalky and pale.

"Who have I become?" the poet asked the water.

But the water didn't answer.

He settled back down into the grass and tried with all his might to write something, anything. He picked up the pen and his fingers began to move slightly, then slowly picked up speed. The words he wrote felt heavy and labored. After his fingers had stopped moving, he read what he had written:

Here I sit
Upon the bank of the lake
Wondering who I am
Not knowing where to go
To find myself.

"I've lost myself," he said after reading his words. His poetry had never sounded so sad, rigid, and uninspired. "My words used to cause people to build monuments, to cook delicacies, to dance wildly, and to accomplish impossible heroic feats. Where is the old magic my words once possessed? Perhaps I've been bewitched?"

That powerful question sat in the silence between him and the lake, begging for an answer. All of a sudden, he began to search the wood for the witches and sorcerers he had heard about in storybooks. He remembered that most of them had pointy hats and small, skinny legs. So, he searched for signs of enchantresses among the bushes. He lost the whole afternoon in his search for the enchanted creatures who could have cast a spell on his words.

He searched and searched. But in the end, he didn't find any pointy hats or skinny legs. The quest only served to make the poet exhausted, and at the end of his search he fell asleep on the boat dock that jutted over the lake. He stretched out beside beautiful, shiny boats moored to the dock and fell into a long, deep sleep. He slept so long, in fact, that many years passed during his slumber.

But one day, the poet woke up in the same exact spot where he had fallen asleep. Only now, the boats that were moored there were dark and unkempt, with torn sails and leaky hulls. He felt uneasy as he rose to his feet.

"What has become of me?" he said as he staggered to his feet and tried to walk the dock. Oddly, there were no people around, only vessels. But stranger still, he didn't feel the need to write anything down at all. It seemed as though the years that had slipped away had also taken away his ability to play with words. Days and weeks passed and still, he thought of nothing to write. He'd become hardened by all the darkness he had experienced, and he could no longer find the lightness and beauty in the world.

All was lost.

But one day, the poet looked out his window and saw something that would change his life forever. He spotted a Thunderbird sitting on the terrace outside his window. The gigantic bird caused the poet to flinch, and he backed away from the window, scared at the sight of the beast. But Naeltim, the sylph of the air, gently opened the poet's window. As the Thunderbird screeched, it turned into a human being.

"Come along now, I don't have much time!" the Thunderbird said.

This was quite possibly the most exciting thing that had ever happened to the young poet. He seemed to shed his sadness in an instant and immediately wished that he had a pen and paper to record this moment when something extraordinary was happening in his life. It gave him the urge to write again.

"Why don't you have much time?" the poet said.

"Because there is only a tiny window, you see, when we recognize the extraordinary things that happen. These moments can't last forever!"

"Why does a mythical bird know such things?"

"Would you stop asking so many questions and come along now?"

The poet leaped out of the window to follow the man who was once a Thunderbird.

"You don't look like you were once such a fearsome bird," the poet said.

"Thank you!" the mysterious man-once-bird said as he began to climb down the ivy of the cottage where the poet lived.

Nervously, the poet placed his foot on the trellis and began to do the same, only much slower, and with much more difficulty.

"Why didn't you just fly down?"

"Because, my dear, I wanted to show you something new," the man-once-bird said.

They quickly ran off together across the great expanse of rolling brown hills and into the countryside. Immediately, the poet's lungs were filled with fresh air.

"That's right, breathe it in and breathe it out!" the man-once-bird said.

"Breathe what in?" the poet asked.

"My goodness, you ask more questions than any other human I've ever met!"

"How many have you known?"

"Well," the man-once-bird wondered aloud as he broke stride and turned to the sky. "Just you!" he said with a laugh.

"Well, that's not many. I mean you don't have anyone to compare me to," the poet said.

"That's because comparison is never good! We are what we are what we are . . ." the man-once-bird said, almost cawing. "Now it's over here, I want you to see this."

They took another path into the forest to a very small shack that the poet never even knew existed.

They slinked around outside of the shack and found a large pile of firewood to hide behind.

"What are we doing here?"

"Shhh. My goodness, you ask so many questions! Stay silent or you will ruin everything!"

The poet shifted in his spot, feeling very uncomfortable as he crouched down so as to not ruin everything.

Soon a gnome—a very ugly gnome—left the shack, followed by a dragon. The dragon was very small but incredibly beautiful. The poet thought that the dragon was quite possibly the most beautiful beast he'd ever seen in his entire life. And in viewing the beauty of the dragon he could feel something shift inside.

The man-once-bird and the poet stayed very, very, very quiet as the ugly gnome and the beautiful dragon picked up a few wicker baskets. They watched the two of them walk over the knoll far to the east, hand in hand, and only then did the man-once-bird shift in his seat.

"What did you see?" the man-once-bird said.

"I saw the most beautiful creature I think I've ever seen in my life!"

"The gnome?"

The poet laughed so hard he almost cried. "No, of course not, silly! The dragon! It's quite obvious that no one would ever think twice about such an ugly gnome."

It had been so many years since the poet had laughed that he actually felt the laughter ripple over his chest, awakening his heart. And somehow, some way, in the laughing he understood the fallacy of what he'd just said. For the laughter awakened compassion within the poet, something that he'd had in very short supply.

"What if I were to tell you that the gnome and the dragon were married?"

"What?! I wouldn't believe you. How could such a beautiful dragon fall in love with such a poor, ugly gnome?"

"Let me tell you a story. Once upon a time, there was a little dragon. She was the most beautiful dragon in all the land, yet she didn't know it. She was just a workhorse dragon used by ogres in their mines to bring out the thing they value most of all."

The poet sat riveted by the man-once-bird's every word. He sat in silence and scarcely had the ability to question anything.

"It is very well known that ogres treasure sunshine most of all, and in order for them to capture as much as possible and bottle it, they need very powerful mirrors made out of obsidian, the blackest gem on earth.

One day, this dragon suffered a terrible injury and cut herself badly on a piece of obsidian. The accident occurred as she was being beaten by the ogres for not bringing up her quota of stone.

She was placed on a heap of sharp obsidian scraps because the ogres had no more use for her. She was simply left there to die. It was there that the poor, ugly gnome found her, nearly drawing her last breath. But the ugly, simple gnome had a special mushroom tonic with him that he had made from his latest forage. The tonic not only healed the cut on the dragon's leg but also brought the dragon out of her purgatory as the life of an ogre's slave and into freedom. As she healed, she became more and more beautiful. She was more herself than she ever had been before."

As the man-once-bird spun the tale, the poet walked around the outside of the shack and spotted a beautiful garden filled with the most beautiful vegetables, fruit, nut trees, and flowers that he'd ever seen. The poet breathed in the lovely scent of a stew simmering on the stove, an enchanting smell that made the poet feel at home, and so yummy it made his tummy grumble. He hadn't eaten in many, many weeks.

"She's the best cook in all the land," the man-once-bird said.

"And to think she was cast on a pile of obsidian scraps and left for dead," the poet said.

"Everything in life changes, my poet friend. You are not any different from the beautiful dragon or anybody else. You are simply going through a process of transformation."

"You think I'm about to become a beautiful dragon?"

The man-once-bird picked a few ripe cherries from the beautiful dragon's cherry tree and handed one to the poet.

Together they took bites of the cherries. "We are all beautiful dragons that have been cast on obsidian scrap heaps," the man-once-bird said.

The poet gorged himself on cherries and after having eaten way too many, he said, "The old me has withered away today. I feel something new has opened my heart and made it less hard than it was this morning. I want to write about the beautiful dragons we are, and about the obsidian scraps we need to leave behind.

As the sun set, the man-once-bird began to turn away from the poet. He walked nervously around in a circle, fearful of turning back into a bird.

"Why did the gnome take such a chance as to anger the ogres? What was it that made him save her?" the poet asked.

"A poem you wrote about love," the man-once-bird said.

"But I haven't written such a poem. I don't know anything about love," the poet insisted.

"You haven't written it . . . yet. These are things that your poetry will do in the future. You are seeing what will be ONLY if you keep writing. Right now, at this very second, the beautiful dragon that you saw here is a slave in the ogres' obsidian mines, just beyond that knoll."

The poet felt more empowered to write now than ever.

"My time is short, but know this: Your poetry is going to mean the difference between life and death in this world. It will cast light in the darkness and inspire many more ugly gnomes to save cast-off dragons."

"Give me a paper and a pen," the poet said.

"I have nothing to offer but this," the man-once bird said.

He handed the poet a stick and pointed to the dirt. As the poet quickly scrawled a poem in the dirt, the man-once-bird said, "The time is now to keep playing with words. Your words will lift people, gnomes, and dragons out of confusion and despair, and do you know why?"

The poet shook his head as he wrote.

"Because they were the afflictions that visited you. Remember this: Focus on the beautiful. Always look for the beautiful."

At dusk, the man disappeared and the Thunderbird returned. He flapped his massive wings and motioned the poet to get on his back for a ride. The poet didn't want to leave the poem he had written in the dirt, but he stepped on to the wing of the Thunderbird, who then slid the poet gently onto his back.

Together, they flew into the sunset.

The gnome soon returned to his home after working at the obsidian mine, exhausted and hungry, his footfalls heavy and plodding. He leaned his dirty steel shovel against his old dilapidated gardening shed. He looked at the awful weeds that had taken over his garden and sighed when he spotted something written in the dirt next to his very tired, very plump feet.

It was a poem:

True beauty
Is a form of
True Love
That nothing can harm
Not its power nor its joy
What?
You say you know not of this kind of love?
Fear not
For you will stop wondering
When it finds you.
When you find you.

STRENGTH

FIRE

How does it transform, I used to wonder
When you were ever so present
And now, my eyes can't see you
And my heart used to ache.
I now see
With the eyes of the soul
And I can tell that you are burning gently
In the flame of my lit candle
While I write all this down,
Flickering gently,
There you are
In my thoughts and through my thoughts
Appearing differently every morning.
And I love you,
My sweet soul.

January 21, 2020
Joshua Tree, California

THE ALBATROSS
AND THE
GIANT RULER

nce upon a time, on the Isle of Tarie Le in the faraway South Pacific, there lived a colony of the largest albatrosses ever, known far and wide as the Wandering Albatrosses of Tarie Le. In every albatross's life, there came a time when they had to leave their parents' nests and travel before returning home to settle and mate. They called this time the Wandering Years. Before returning home to make their own nests, they enjoyed eight years of exploration and adventures around the globe.

Albatrosses can soar for years and can also sleep as they fly, so they can make the longest voyages of any bird species. On their journeys, they encountered flocks of birds and creatures they'd never met before who helped them understand the world and their place in it. They also learned things they never knew before, including how to survive storms and how to soar over the oceans without ever touching land.

The young albatross, Omar, did not differ from the other one-year-old chicks. He spent his early years learning how to fly farther and farther, and he learned how to adapt to his ever-expanding wings. On his fourth birthday, the perfect age for embarking on his adventure, Omar reached a great wingspan of twelve feet, perfect for gliding over the oceans. This incurred no danger at all, since Omar would almost always be in flight.

Over the years, Omar had watched as fellow albatrosses took off on their wonderful voyages, but when the day arrived for him to fly away, he became frightened about going out into the world all alone. He loved the nest he shared with his family and he didn't want to believe the terrible stories he'd heard about other birds getting entangled or hooked in the fishing gear of mighty ships. He wondered what he would do if he ran into the same fate. Nothing scared him more than flying near one of the huge, looming fishing boats.

"Never ever fly near the very large ships. And if you must, only do it during the daytime. At night there are powers in the air and in the sea that we do not understand. Never fly around those ships unless you are with another albatross," Omar's father said. They were the last words he spoke to Omar before his voyage.

Omar knew that it was time for him to begin his Wandering Years. He couldn't afford to waste any more time on land. He had to become brave and strong enough to take his first long wing flaps and practice his soaring and gliding. Naeltim, the sylph of the air, blew a cool but gentle wind, propelling Omar out of his nest and onto a gentle breeze. This is how Omar's Wandering Years started, and they would take him across the vast expanse of ocean.

Omar took a big breath and let it out. It calmed him to think how about brave he would become if he survived the journey. He thought about his nest on the Isle of Tarie Le. At night, while he was flying over the ocean, he dreamed about his future life on the island and all the wisdom he would gain during his Wandering Years. He dreamed of the beautiful girlfriend he would meet. And he dreamed of returning to her each night, to the nest they'd build together, where they would have their own chicks and help them find the courage to go on their own journeys.

More than ever, he wished that he didn't have to make the arduous and perilous journey. But with the dream of his future family in his head, he kept his beak up as he soared higher into the air and farther from his home. Years of travel went by, and on one clear day he spotted something huge, like a small village moving in the water below.

The Giant Ruler was the biggest ship at sea. Omar sniffed the air in its wake. Tempting smells came from the decks of the boat where they cleaned and processed cod, and then sent the fillets into a holding tank. A long stream of albacore, cod, minnows, and squid flooded the water off the stern of the ship. He couldn't help but become lured by their tasty scents. He'd been flying for so long at sea that he'd forgotten to eat for many days. The ocean had a way of hypnotizing him to the point where he lost all track of time.

In fact, after all these years of travel, Omar had become an especially adventurous albatross. He had not only become accustomed to the oceans and all their majestic nooks and crannies, but he also experimented with going places where his family had told him not to, like the inside of sea caves. But during his Wandering Years, he had learned valuable lessons about the tides and knew that with the right tide, there was no danger at all. More and more, the world's great beauty surrounded Omar, and little by little he understood her mysteries and let go of his fear.

When Omar swooped low over the water to scoop an albacore out of the water, he got caught up in the wake of the Giant Ruler and discovered he couldn't fly like he usually did. He remembered his father's last words to him. At that moment, when he started flailing and descending into a corkscrew twist, something happened that he never felt before. Suddenly he saw more clearly and could count the number of hands on deck. He even saw that they had their spyglasses set on him.

Although Omar didn't know it, the powerful Great Siren of the Seas had given a special power to Omar because of his natural curiosity. The Siren wanted him to become the next Great Investigator so that one day, he would return to inform the other albatrosses about new dangers lurking out there in the world and impart the wisdom he had gained on his many adventures. Every eight years, the Great Siren bestowed this unique power onto the young albatross who was the most nervous and the most curious. But they never realized they were the next Great Investigator until they returned home.

Omar looked to his left, and he looked to his right, and he didn't see his wings. He looked down to his albatross feet and didn't see a trace of himself anywhere in the air.

"What has happened to me? What is going on?" Omar shouted.

He swooped down low to the Giant Ruler and flew above the boat to see more of the world of men. Many birds had gotten caught in their traps. He flew on to see lots and lots of discarded plastic in the ocean. He gasped in horror. Over the years, he saw many similar fishing boats and lots of birds trapped in their nets amid a myriad of plastic and garbage.

This angered Omar so much that he abandoned his Wandering Years to dedicate himself to warning his fellow birds. Day by day, he gathered not only the courage but also the wisdom to warn every bird he could.

First, he tried yelling at the birds, "Turn around, stay away from the fishing boats below! You will get entangled in their nets and die! Go back!"

But his voice wasn't that strong, and most birds never paid attention. So, he had to come up with another way. He swept down just above the fading wake of the large fishing boats, and because of his size—much larger than albatrosses of his age and one hundred times larger than any seagoing bird— they paid attention, especially when he discovered how to fly upside down.

"Turn around, stay away from the fishing boats below—you will get entangled in their nets and die! Go back!" Omar said.

"What are you doing? Birds aren't meant to fly that way?" a very superior seagull said.

"Don't fly that way! Fly due north and save yourself!" Omar yelled.

"Whatever do you mean? I've never flown this way before and I want to see the world," the seagull snapped.

"Do so at your own peril," Omar said.

The snooty seagull ignored Omar's warning and flew on.

Omar wanted to follow the snooty seagull and try to save him one more time, but there were many more birds to save. He began flying upside down once more. It's very uncomfortable to do the thing that you always have done upside down or backward, but Omar decided it was the only way to save the most birds possible.

He saved many, many birds that day. But he couldn't get the snooty seagull out of his mind. So, he became invisible and flew very close to the fishing boat, skimming the top of the ocean to see if he could spot the bird. And there below Omar, floating in the water and sandwiched between a bottle of laundry detergent and a toy doll, the snooty seagull was trapped with a net around his neck.

"No one should die this way!" Omar shouted out.

And he swooped down to where the snooty seagull lay gasping. He flipped upside down and used his beak as scissors to cut the seagull out. Snip. Snip. Snip. The seagull was free! But he couldn't fly anymore, and so Omar placed the seagull on some driftwood floating in the ocean. The snooty seagull was frightened because he didn't enjoy floating in the water very much, and he couldn't see who'd saved him until Omar reappeared, just above beside the seagull.

"Why did you risk your life for a snooty seagull like me?"

"Because it is my responsibility to help as many birds as I can," Omar said. "Just wait here and I'll have the other seagulls take you home."

"Thank you," the seagull said, no longer snooty. "I should have paid attention."

Omar smiled. "Sometimes it's hard to hear what we don't want to hear."

The seagull relaxed, taking a seat on the driftwood and sunning himself while floating on the gentle ripple of the ocean. Omar flew into the afternoon sun and told some oncoming seagulls about their friend in need. He spotted the seagulls landing beside the formerly snooty seagull on the debris field of driftwood in the ocean before they all took flight together.

Over the years, Omar became the guardian of the South Pacific, and he saved thousands and thousands of birds from certain entrapment and death. And yet, with every mission, he thought about his dream girl and settling down. And after eight long years at sea, his wings had gotten weary, and it was time to think about flying home. His Wandering Years had ended nobly.

When he finally landed in the mating colony, he met his future wife, Princess Morness. Her father, the king, had requested an audience with Omar to grant him the title of Great Investigator, the great honor the Siren of the Seas had bestowed upon him secretly long ago. This came as a shock to Omar, for he didn't feel that he had done anything any other albatross wouldn't do under the circumstances. He was a special albatross and didn't even know it.

"Because of your incredible deeds and bravery despite your fear of the unknown, I give you this medal," the king said.

As the king pinned the medal onto Omar, his eyes met with Princess Morness. He'd never seen a beauty such as hers. Her feathers were impossibly white, and she had a sparkle in her eye he'd never seen before. Yet it seemed like he'd known her forever. Soon they married on the remote side of Isle of Tarie Le and built their treehouse there. They had twenty little albatrosses who grew into big albatrosses, and who all went on their own Wandering Years and accomplished incredible things on their own. But they never left before their father had given them a word of advice: "You are never alone. Your mom and I will always be with you in your heart."

CONFIDENCE

GLOW

It is not always easy
Not seeing you anymore
Through my eyes
I no longer see you
And all of my other senses
Have ceased to have you near
As much as they have ceased to have you far.
I'm aching
And the other day
I burned in the confusion of it all
As your love surrounds me deeply
Enveloping me in your wings
As I move along the Path
You whisper Words of Wisdom
That Keep me Safe and Sound.
Joy and Pain
Are my Friends now
As I move along the Path
Trying to understand
Although I know that it will all Pass
And that one day I will be Stripped of the
Confusion
While Basking in the Glow of your Being.

February 21, 2020
Mountain Center, Southern California

THE SHEIK
AND THE
GOLDEN EGG

 jolly old man lived in a house constructed of his own homemade butterscotch candy, encircled by a candy cane fence with a driveway made of strawberry taffy. Colorful little jellybeans decorated the butterscotch walls and roof of his home. But it was his cotton candy chimney that made all the people in the neighborhood stop and stare on their evening and morning strolls, especially on frosty days when he had a fire going. The scent from his cotton candy smoke made everyone in Huckleberry Hill hungry for their favorite sweet.

"Have you ever seen such a sight?!" one neighbor said to the other.

"Not in all my life," the neighbor replied.

Glorious details like golden unicorn statues and lemonade-scented flowers greeted admirers of the jolly old man's home and grounds. From early in the morning until late at night, fun sing-along music wafted from the living room, where a player piano played cheerful ragtime music. Out on the perfectly manicured lawn, the jolly old man had gigantic chess, checkers, and tic-tac-toe pieces set up for the neighborhood children whenever they stopped over.

He loved his butterscotch and cotton candy creations, especially his garage. He'd carefully constructed it out of gigantic Twizzlers in such a way that it appeared to be a log cabin, with rich, melted white chocolate acting as mortar and holding the Twizzlers together. Long, long ago, the jolly old man had sold all of his possessions and given away what didn't sell, so he was free to create a place that reflected the jolly state of his heart.

Over the garage, the old man had placed a handmade wooden sign that read "Toy Store." Inside this delicious place, he invited the poor children of Huckleberry Hill to come eat the walls, and they happily accepted his invitation. This made him a very busy jolly old man, for every night he'd have to reconstruct the toy store after the children had had their fill of candy. But lucky for him, the most marvelous and very busy dragonflies helped him reconstruct the store at night, so every day it looked perfectly beautiful again for the poor children who wanted to come to nibble.

Every day he invited the same poor children to pick one toy from the sea of toys he had handmade for them. He enjoyed making toy robots, dolls, colorful cities out of Playdough, the most refined construction sets, and even water slides in the shapes of his favorite animals. Each day, when each child selected the one toy they loved most of all, their gleeful smiles filled him with joy.

Children of all ages came from miles around to eat the walls and play with the toys at the toy store. Not one child ever left with anything other than a gigantic smile on their face. But the jolly old man had a smile bigger and brighter than any of the children because he took all the money he had and spent it on creating unique toys so that the poor children living around Huckleberry Hill could have a special toy all their own.

But his home and the toy store required constant care, and more and more children came over the years. Even with the dragonflies helping every night, he needed to do many repairs himself, and he continued to manufacture more and more toys for the boys and girls after selling out each day, so he rarely slept. Nighttime was when his creative energy took flight, and he would work in his basement workshop, busily hammering away on his newest creations. Each toy was one-of-a-kind and, therefore, a collector's item. He wanted every child to feel special and feel that the toy had been not just selected by them but also was made especially for them. When the children held the old man's toys in their arms and had his candy in their bellies, he could sense their joy, and that's what made him so jolly day after day and night after night.

But one day, a little boy entered the toy store. He didn't have an appetite, and so he didn't eat the walls. He didn't care about toys, and so he didn't pick any.

"What is wrong, my son? Why are you not hungry?" the jolly old man asked.

"I don't know," the little boy replied.

"And why do you not play with the other children?" the jolly old man asked.

The little boy just shrugged his shoulders.

"Now then, let's just sit together for a while. Do you know any jokes?" the jolly old man asked.

"Not really, what is a joke?" the little boy asked.

"A joke is something that makes us laugh. It's a play on words, it's a funny story," the jolly old man said. "Do you know a funny story?"

"Yes," the little boy said with a tiny grin. "There was a jolly old man who made a house out of candy!" The little boy's tiny grin turned into an enormous smile. The boy laughed and the jolly old man laughed too!

Then some children from Huckleberry Hill gathered around to see what the jolly old man was up to, because he had laughed so very hard that his voice carried clear across the valley. Soon, many other children from many villages were playing with his child-sized games. The place was overflowing with children. On that day, the children had totally gobbled up the toy store and exhausted his supply of handmade toys. Still, the jolly old man had the most enormous smile on his face.

That night, he summoned an army of dragonflies and enlisted the help of child-sized toy soldiers to help with both the construction of the toy store, and also with making toys for the next day's fun.

The following day, the jolly old man got the surprise of his life. The entire town and some neighboring villages brought their kids over to the toy store, not to eat and select toys, but to give the jolly old man candy and give him gifts of new tools and bunches of strawberry-scented flowers because it was his birthday. He had turned one hundred two years old after the clock had struck midnight, and the village turned into a huge party. There were root beer floats and hot-air balloon rides and child-sized toy cars that the children raced over gumdrop tracks. At the day's end, the candy cane fence around the jolly old man's home set off fireworks into the sky that rained candy down into the waiting arms of the children.

Across the street, a grumpy old miser lived in a brick house surrounded by iron gates with huge stone pillars. He had barricaded himself behind his mansion walls with all the money he'd earned raising and selling majestic peacocks. The majestic peacocks were special in that, twice a year, they would lay eggs made of solid gold. He would sell the golden eggs to the sheiks in the Middle East, who showcased them in their grandiose palaces. As you may imagine, the golden eggs were very profitable, and the grumpy old miser had become very rich. However, as he became rich, his world became smaller and smaller and smaller. Eventually he was worth so much money that he never left the four walls of his bunker-like home, because he was afraid that someone might kidnap him and demand all his money as ransom and discover his majestic peacocks.

Because of his paranoia, the grumpy old miser's appearance became very scary. He became unrecognizable to the people who had once loved him, and as he became more and more cruel to them, they stopped visiting—which was just fine by the grumpy old miser. He didn't like the energy it took to be nice, and so he didn't care for meeting people at all. His disheveled gray hair smelled like a basement filled with cobwebs, and even his skin looked grey. The only thing that gave him any pleasure at all was to count his money and to witness the laying of the golden eggs.

The grumpy miser kept the majestic peacocks in small cages in his basement until he had verified the buyer's claims of his sheikdom and vast fortunes. At the time of a sale, he would dress nicely and pretend to be just like the jolly old man, acting sweetly to the purchasers, even handing them candy so they wouldn't suspect his greediness and cruelty. He even placed plants and flowers in the only windowsill he had to welcome his customers, who were his only guests.

The majestic peacocks cried for help in the basement, because the grumpy old man was too miserly to keep them in anything but tiny, cramped cages where the birds could barely stand. They had no room at all to spread their beautiful tail feathers. How the majestic peacocks wished someone would save them from their awful existence. Nothing hurt worse than the day they delivered their golden eggs, because that meant they had to stand up straight and spread their gorgeous plumes into the cold, hard, steel cages.

Year after year, egg by egg, and one by one, their gorgeous tail feathers fell to the ground. This made the grumpy old miser happy because it gave him a side hustle of selling majestic peacock feathers too. And nothing, absolutely nothing in the world, made him as happy as making more money. To end their misery, the peacocks all decided to shout loudly, all at the same time, the next time a visitor came. They hoped this would work well because the grumpy old miser was also hard of hearing.

One day, in the middle of an afternoon spent eating the toy store and playing with their toys, the children heard noises coming from the basement of the grumpy old miser and wondered what was going on. Later that afternoon, the grumpy old miser was planning to sell yet another golden egg to the one of most powerful sheiks of all. The sheik had traveled the world in search of the most beautiful golden eggs to decorate the majestic tomb of his beloved young wife. When the sheik had finished investigating the authenticity of the egg, Naeltim, the sylph of the air, pushed the basement door open.

At first the sheik only heard the wretched cries of the majestic peacocks, which yet again fell on the grumpy old miser's deaf ears. Then, an awful smell came from the basement, worse than the smell of one hundred skunks spraying, which terrified the sheik. The grumpy old miser had gotten accustomed to the smell during his harvesting of golden eggs. When the sheik investigated the basement over the protests of the grumpy old miser, he saw the unthinkable conditions of the precious birds. The only thing that shone in the darkness was a fresh golden egg, which sat beneath a crying majestic peacock as its last tailfeather floated to the filthy, slimy ground. The sheik screamed in terror. The birds screeched in utter despair.

The sheik was not only powerful but also a wonderful man who loved children. In fact, he so mourned the loss of the children he would never have with his beloved wife that he had set up hundreds of toy shops where jolly men made toys for the poor children of his country. Terrified, surprised, and anguished, the sheik immediately understood the calamity of the majestic peacocks. So, he kept his cool when he proposed to buy not just the golden egg but ALL the peacocks from the grumpy old miser.

"But these are the ONLY majestic peacocks that exist! How will I sell any more golden eggs if you buy all the peacocks?" said the grumpy old miser.

"After I buy the golden egg and all the majestic peacocks, you will be the richest man in this hemisphere, and you won't have to worry about selling the eggs anymore," said the sheik.

The grumpy old miser agreed, but only after calculating in his mind all the money that he would have made. When the sale was completed after the simple press of a few buttons on the sheik's phone, the grumpy old miser's eyes fired up with greed. He'd have more money than he could store in any of his safes at his bunker-like home. Pondering how many more safes he would need to construct made the miser fabulously happy.

When the sheik left the grumpy old miser's military estate, he immediately walked across the street and donated the golden egg to the jolly old man, who sold it to make money so he could continue to make more toys and properly reconstruct his toy shop every day after the children had nibbled away at its Twizzler log cabin walls.

The jolly old man adopted the majestic peacocks, who roamed around freely in his backyard and loved to play with the children who visited.

One day, everyone needed to seek shelter from a powerful storm brought on by Naeltim, the sylph of the air. Everyone was secure in their homes because they had had plenty of warning. But when the terrible tempest had passed, it had left nothing of the bunker-like estate of the grumpy old miser. The storm had demolished his home and swept up his money, which slowly fell back to earth into the hands of the poor children. And no one in the village ever saw the grumpy old miser again.

GLOW

FOR YOU

Because time is just an illusion
And this moment is forever
I remember you as Forever
And Forever is not only in my Little Heart
It sits right now in front of me
In all that I do
Because from now on all that I do is for You
Because you are in everything
And Everything is Connected
And the Beauty of You
Is the Beauty of Everything
In those Once lost Souls, I find you
Because those lost Souls Will be no more
They Will Be Safe
And their Glow Will be Brighter than all the Stars
Combined.
Because I love you,
I also Love them
And it's all clear now
As all the Lessons and Motions and Processes
Have always shown me their Way at the
Right time.

February 26, 2020
Mountain Center, Southern California

NAVAJO TRAIN
AND BALD EAGLE

avajo Train, a proud passenger train on the Atchison, Topeka, and Santa Fe Railway, sped out of Chicago. All the passengers aboard the No. 9 were thrilled to take the ride out west. In three days, they would be transported to the West Coast via Topeka, St. John, and Pasadena, making three meal stops each day.

The year was 1939. One night, on the longest day of the year, the passengers left during an early snowfall in the Windy City for the sunny skies of Los Angeles. It would take them almost sixty hours to arrive where their hearts desired to be, where some would choose to stay for the rest of their lives.

While most of the passengers slept, Navajo Train chug-chug-chugged along during a full moon that started rising after the last finger of sunshine passed into darkness. At exactly this moment, Bald Eagle tried to race Navajo Train. The train was very lonely and welcomed the company. For a while, he had been widely and publicly heralded for a job well done because of his dependable speed and economical comfort. But even with all the accolades, he was always lonely, even though his train cars were always sold out, full of people from all over the world.

Somewhere in the vast wilderness of the American West, Navajo Train noticed Bald Eagle not only racing him but also trying to fly as high as the moon! Navajo Train watched Eagle soar up and up and up. And just when Navajo Train thought the noble bird couldn't possibly fly any higher, he would watch Eagle soar down, down, down, and practically skim the steel of his train cars. None of the passengers ever knew that the train and the bird had begun a wonderful friendship.

"Aren't you afraid of flying so high, Eagle?"

"I have been following your route every day," Eagle said, "and you seem to constantly do the same thing. Aren't you tired of always doing the same thing? You seem to go back and forth from the same place to the other place. Aren't you afraid of becoming bored?"

Navajo Train didn't know the meaning of the word "bored" and spent the next few miles on his travel contemplating this idea.

"What in the world does 'bored' mean?" Navajo Train finally said.

"It means when you do the same thing all the time. It means there is no adventure. There is nothing interesting or new!" Eagle said.

"Every day is a new adventure for me, actually," Navajo Train said, filled with pride. "I bring great joy to the world and a quick journey to travelers. I have been following the same route because it's the most scenic in all of America. I am the train the people have made. Why, only today I just met you, my very first friend."

As their friendship grew over the years, Eagle gained wisdom from the proud, aging train. They always had their longest conversations in the evenings when there was a full moon and during the long, sunny, summer days when they were able to see each other best. And as the train aged, it became harder and harder for Navajo Train to really see Eagle. He knew his shrill whistle, though, and that always resulted in Navajo Train's speed jumping just a little bit more than it had before, like a quickening heartbeat when someone you love is near. On those nights, the travelers reached their destination two hours earlier than the scheduled arrival.

During their journeys together, Eagle would ask Navajo Train about many things, especially about getting old. It was the thing Eagle feared the most, especially the idea of losing his eyesight like Navajo Train. That meant death for older bald eagles, who then became easy prey. "Is it hard getting old?" Eagle asked, years after the first night they met.

Eagle had become faster and faster, and sometimes on evenings where the wind wasn't too strong, he would even fly to the front engine of Navajo Train so that his friend could see him clearly. Besides, he loved flying faster than Navajo Train! Nothing made him happier than to fly right at the nose of the train so they could talk all night long. And nothing made Navajo Train happier than getting a good look at his special and only friend.

Navajo Train put off answering his friend's important question until one night, when Eagle asked yet again. "Some things are harder, but most things get easier. I appreciate my beautiful life more and my strong engine. As I get older, I feel like I become more and more myself. Happy with what is," Navajo Train said.

"I don't ever want to be happy with what is! I always want to catch a bigger snake and fly faster and faster and faster. I don't think I'll ever be happy with what is. I always want more!"

"Is 'more' better?" Navajo Train asked.

"Yes, of course, it is! I like going higher and higher and higher and faster and faster and faster. I don't know how you enjoy doing the same thing all the time, day after day, year after year," Eagle said.

"Promise me something," Navajo Train said.

"What?"

"One day, when I'm old and gone and you are still flying higher and faster and racing some other train, promise me . . ." Navajo Train said.

"I'll never race another train, we're friends—I can't just be friends with any train. Anyways, you're the fastest train there is! Why would I want to race a freight train?!" Eagle said.

"Promise me that when the time comes and another train comes along, you'll learn to enjoy your own speed, and never judge your happiness by the speed of others or by beating the train," Navajo Train said.

"You're silly!"

Over the years, the eagle and the train got to know each other pretty well. Eagle always wished that the train could live his life off the rails so that he could truly understand the freedom Eagle enjoyed. And Navajo Train wished that his friend would learn the peace of not having to worry about the route taken and just surrender to the beauty of the passing scenery and the nuances of how each trip was different, even if the path was the same.

Then one day, everything changed. Eagle didn't swoop up as high or as low as he had before. He stayed close to the nose of Navajo Train and didn't want to leave him.

"What's the matter, my friend?" Navajo Train said, because friends know such things. Friends don't have to tell each other that something is wrong.

It took a while for Eagle to offer his reply.

"When I fly really high and then swoop really low to the Earth, I have noticed many things," Bald Eagle said.

"Good for you, that's marvelous. What have you noticed?!" Navajo Train asked, happy that Eagle might have come to know the peace of simply enjoying the ride, instead of swooping and dropping so fast and so much all the time.

"Well, what I saw wasn't marvelous at all," Eagle said.

Navajo Train silently moved, waiting for his friend to tell him in his own time.

"They excavated some land. It's a huge area of land where there is going to be a new village. New families of humans are moving into the new houses that have been constructed there even now. And worst of all . . ." Eagle got choked up. He didn't know how to say what he had to say next.

"Well, out with it my friend, go ahead," Navajo Train said.

"A new railway is being built, Navajo Train."

"How is that possible! A new railway? How can they build a NEW railway? Especially when this one is so well-traveled and adored? It would be folly! How confusing I would find it to take a different route. Are you sure, Eagle? Maybe you saw something else?"

"I assure you, Navajo Train, it is true. It makes me sad too. They're building a new railway. I swooped down low and heard the engineers talking. They say the new railway will be ready very soon. I can see it perfectly with my perfect eyesight when I am flying high above everything."

They went a long way together, with Eagle flying at the nose of Navajo Train's engine for miles and miles in silence.

"And what will happen with the old railway, Eagle? Will it still be in use? How long will the new railway be? How many locomotives will there be? How many routes will there be? Tell me, Eagle!"

"I do not know such things, except what I can see. I assure you, Navajo Train, that it will be a very long and sophisticated railway. They are building everything from scratch, and there will be many, many, many routes on the new railway. They're also rolling out many new locomotives; in fact, every locomotive will be new."

"Every one?"

Eagle didn't reply.

"I thought we would travel the west together forever, Navajo Train . . ." Eagle said. "I guess we don't know how long it will last."

"Not much longer?" Navajo Train asked.

"No," Eagle replied.

"What a lucky train I am to have a friend like you," Navajo Train said.

"But this isn't lucky at all, it's terrible!" Eagle said.

"But you have given me the gift of knowing! You aren't afraid of going up high or plummeting low because that's what eagles do. Because of you, I get to enjoy every day we have together more than I ever would have before. Thank you, Eagle. Thank you for being such a great friend. I will always treasure our adventures together," Navajo Train said.

"We only have the rest of this season, that's what the engineer said," Eagle replied.

There was more silence between them as they stared at the impossibly beautiful full moon. On any other evening, Navajo Train would have watched Bald Eagle soar into the moon's silver light. He missed seeing Eagle swirl and swoop.

"Whatever is the matter, Eagle?"

"I don't feel like swooping anymore," Eagle said.

"But why?" Navajo Train said. "Please swoop and plummet, for I love watching you so!"

And with that, the bald eagle put on the best show ever. He swooped higher and soared longer in the moonlight than ever before. It was something Navajo Train would remember for the rest of his life.

"Train, I don't want to think of you dismissed and mothballed to some old ratty train station where you will rust and your windows will break. I want to be by your side, just like this, forever and ever."

"Don't you think that would be boring?" Navajo Train asked.

They both laughed.

Navajo Train was retired to the railway yard by the train station just outside of Topeka. And the friendship between Navajo Train and Eagle grew even deeper even after that. Every night, Eagle told Navajo Train about all the exciting happens in the world from the new tracks that he would never travel.

And Eagle soared beside Navajo Train, even though his friend could only see Eagle flying high in his imagination.

NEW HEIGHTS

STARLIGHT

In the evening, my sweet baby,

When you are set for bed,

Look out your window,

Because there are lots of stars.

They sure are beautiful to look at,

And believe me, there are

Way more than one thousand!

They make up the whole sky,

And the sky is huge.

Just think of how lucky you are

To look at all the stars!

But, also, the stars are lucky to look at you!

Because, you know what?

Without you,

The stars would not even exist,

And they are so happy that you are there

for them, too!

There are lots and lots of stars, out there in

the sky!

One of his favorite stories

STARLIGHT

nce upon a time, a beautiful star named Earal was the brightest, most captivating star of all. She had become really good friends with an eight-year-old boy who lived in Ethiopia, named Geneyanesh.

He had met her one night when he was very sad. He'd been working hard to take care of his sick mother and father and didn't know what to do. Finally, when they were fast asleep and so were his other brothers and sisters, the little boy snuck outside and knelt down to pray. But he became distracted by the most beautiful sight he'd ever seen. He'd often wandered the savannah at night to find their escaped goat or to help his dad take care of their animals when he was unwell. Now, all those tasks were left to Geneyanesh. But never, not one time, had he seen such a star.

"How did I ever miss you?" Geneyanesh said.

"Many people do. But I'm here now and so happy to know you, Geneyanesh," she said.

"What do I do now?" Geneyanesh said. "My parents are so sick; I don't know what to do."

"Go to sleep; I'll be with you. I'll see you in your dreams," she said.

So he did. And she was with him in his dreams.

Each night afterward, Geneyanesh would leave his home and walk up the tallest hillside, take a seat, and speak with Earal. He wanted to be as close as possible to her because he wanted to be sure she could hear him well enough. They talked to each other every night about many things, and Earal answered many of Geneyanesh's questions like, *Why do little boys have to stay home and take care of their sick parents? Why do so many people he knows have to die? Why are zebras striped? And why couldn't his little sister stop bugging him to help her bring water from the river every day?*

It didn't take long for Geneyanesh to become very wise for his tender age.

But during the day, when Geneyanesh milked the goats or helped his sister retrieve the water in the early morning hours, he wished he could talk with his best friend Earal. He was very excited to see her at night because he had so many more questions for her. Things in their village didn't make sense to Geneyanesh, like why the hospital didn't have mosquito nets or beds and why medicine never came. He also wanted to know what to do about helping his neighbor, Akeesha, make enough food for all her brothers and sisters.

But that night, Geneyanesh couldn't see Earal. He ran and ran throughout the savannah, trying to find her. Every star in the sky was there, it seemed, except for her. He ran to the very top of the hill where they used to talk and laugh. And she wasn't there. Not anywhere. So, he wouldn't get the answers he needed that night. And he cried himself to sleep.

He felt abandoned, and the next day he didn't feel like getting the water from the well, or taking care of his sick parents, or milking the goat, or even helping Akeesha make enough food for all her brothers and sisters. He still did those things, but as a shell of who he once was. Beauty had left the world.

The village elder noticed a change in the little boy. And the elder asked Geneyanesh to go into the savannah with him to watch the elephants at the watering hole that night. The little boy didn't want to go. He didn't care about elephants. He'd seen a million of them and he thought they were stinky and loud.

But the elder convinced him, saying that if Geneyanesh came, he would find what he was looking for. *How could that be?* the little boy thought. *The elder doesn't know about my best friend.* He didn't know that the elder *did* know about Earal and wanted to help. But because Geneyanesh loved and missed Earal so much, he went along with the elder's request. Giving up precious hours of sleep to speak with Earal was one thing, but giving up his precious hours of sleep to accompany some old man he hardly knew into the savannah to watch stupid elephants was another. He dragged his feet, and it took them twice as long as it should have to reach the watering hole.

They both hunkered down in the rocks and grass close to the water.

"Just like your special star, elephants have a very unique appearance," the elder said. "No other animal in the world has long trunk noses, large floppy ears, and thick wide legs."

"You know about my special star?" asked Geneyanesh. "No other star in the universe sparkles as brightly and as beautifully as Earal. She was my best friend," the little boy said.

"What else do you see here? What else can you tell me about the elephants?" the elder asked.

"They like to get dirty," the little boy said at the sight of some of the little elephants rolling and playing at the watering hole.

"They love to play," the elder said.

"I love to play too," the little boy said.

"Elephants instantly love their children at birth, at first sight. I believe that is the same type of love you share with Earal," the elder said.

"How do you know her name?" the little boy asked.

"Because once a very long time ago, she spoke with me," he said.

The boy couldn't believe it.

"I've seen you at night on the highest hill. And I know you found great comfort there," the elder said. "When I was a little boy, I once went to the same hill."

There was a sacred silence as the two watched the elephants drink and play.

"Did you know elephants can do something else that is truly extraordinary?"

"What?" the little boy asked. His eyes went wide.

"Elephants love each other so much that they can communicate with each other even when they can't see each other."

"Really? How?"

"They use low-pitched sounds that fall below the audible range of humans, and they can talk to each other up to two miles away," the elder said.

The little boy turned to look at the elephants. "But they never leave each other. They never just disappear," the little boy said.

"The stars appear to us as if they are never moving, and yet, they are in a cosmic dance. As the Earth rotates, the stars change their position in the sky," the elder said. "They sometimes leave our sight, but they never disappear. They simply move on to another part of the world as the seasons change."

"I don't like that change. I miss her and I want to talk to her every night," the little boy said.

"She knows that. That's why she's like the elephants. You may not see her, but she's still there in the heavens above, and she's able to communicate with you. She has that ability," the elder said.

"How?"

"Because she no longer lives in the sky, you see? She lives in your heart," the elder said, placing his hand over Geneyanesh's heart.

"So how do I talk to her now?"

"The same way you always have; at night when your family is asleep, go to the hill and you will see," the elder said.

"But she will be too far away, I won't be able to hear her," the little boy said.

"She's closer than ever before. She's right here," the elder said, pointing to the little boy's heart.

Geneyanesh smiled. "That means I can talk to her whenever I want? That means that I can tell her things on the walk home from the water well with my sister, and when I help Akeesha make enough food for all her brothers and sisters, and when I milk the goat?"

The elder smiled and nodded his head. "Yes, and then one day, Naeltim, the sylph of the air, will blow his soft wind, rotating the Earth again so that you, my dear Geneyanesh, and your best friend Earal, will see each other again."

TOGETHERNESS

THE LIGHT

You Used to Feel so Alone
Trying to maintain a balance between being
Yourself and Fitting into the World
Alone, you Woke up, and Alone, you Went About
your Day,
Trying to so desperately figure out the Hows, the
Whys and the Wheres
The Motives Behind it All,
But, especially, the Roadmap of your own Hero's
Journey.
And Yet, there was always a Bright Light Inside of
You
That You could have Accessed at Any Time
To become Stronger, to Explore
A Light that Shone Brighter than You could have
Ever Imagined
A Light that I will Never Forget,
And A Light that Will keep on Shining over the
World.
On Earth, I will create the Most Beautiful Dream
And This Dream Will be the Biggest Dreams of All
A Dream of Peace, Love and Joy,
And Your Name Will be Written all Over it.

April 25, 2020
Idyllwild, Southern California

THE PRIESTESS
IN THE TEMPLE
OF RHYMES

 priestess named Amalthea lived in a tucked-away temple. Her parents gave their beautiful daughter the sweet name because it described her soft, soothing spirit. As she grew up, she spoke in rhymes, which had the enchanting effect of taking every worry and every stress away from anyone within earshot. Soon, everyone from the Kingdom of Fataguro flocked to the temple to listen to the priestess's beautiful rhyming poems.

Since the temple was tucked away, her voice was the only way pilgrims could find her. But because the temple was situated on a high cliff where the winds whipped loudly, sometimes they became confused about which way to go. Once the pilgrims had hiked to the top of the cliff, a special glow illuminated the forest outside of the temple walls and helped guide them to the temple, even on the stormiest of nights. With every step the pilgrims took as they traversed the cliff, their curiosity grew about the source of the supernatural light.

With great joy, they spotted the incredible temple that had been built into the very trees of the forest. The temple servants had braided golden ribbons into the leaves of every tree, and the priestess's royal flags displayed her crest as they waved from the tops of the four gigantic trees that defined the temple's perimeter.

A giant golden chain dangled at the temple door. To gain entry, the pilgrims used all their strength to ring the ancient bell in the belfry. Upon the dulcet ring of the bell, temple servants opened huge golden doors, and the pilgrims walked inside under the inscription "Amoris Lingua," which means "the language of love." When they entered the chamber, the pilgrims had to shield their eyes because they weren't used to the light of unconditional love that emanated from Amalthea whenever she sat on her throne and spoke to those assembled.

Her long, soft, blue hair framed a face full of grace. The temple smelled of jasmine and roses and instantly calmed the most nervous listeners. Her genuine, passionate, and optimistic spirit created a special glow that shone from her glittering skin. Amalthea made herself available as long as the people of the kingdom wanted to listen to her rhymes, often until the wee hours of the morning. Once they had learned her simple but subtle language, they discovered that while her wisdom was easy to remember, it was not always easy to implement. But as the pilgrims understood her and took action in their lives toward unconditional love, her wisdom would guide them forever.

However, the intimate temple experience involved much more than mere listening. The pilgrims became enthralled with the language the priestess created. She spoke in only rhyme, and yet her rhymes were also like puzzles. It was the listener's job to understand and decipher her important messages. Her poems were very simple, but because most people had become so burdened by everyday encumbrances and problems, their comprehension of language and ways of being in the world became convoluted and confusing. They had lost their way and no longer knew what really mattered, and so they had to unlearn many things.

Yet things hadn't always been peaceful for Amalthea. For as bright as her glow was, her darkness had once been greater. She had lost her daughter in the forest many years ago and never found her. Although her grief was great, her love for her daughter was constant and infinite and surpassed the cavernous ache she felt inside after the disappearance. Naeltim, the sylph of the air, had blown her confusion away. And in the days and years afterward, Amalthea learned much about infinite love, which is simple and has no boundaries. She built the temple in her daughter's honor so that others could learn how to care for themselves and not succumb to the snares of confusion, pain, anger, and regret.

But a greater darkness had settled like a storm cloud over the kingdom in the years after the young girl's disappearance. No one understood how such a tragedy could occur in their beautiful part of the world. The people who heard about the tragedy became confused and lost their way. Life became contorted and difficult. Because their hearts hardened and they rarely spoke to each other, the people lost their ability to understand each other and express themselves. The kingdom slowly descended into chaos. Villagers lost all sense of self and the ability to have gratitude for the simple, genuine, and authentic.

And so, like players in the great dramas of the stage, the people of the kingdom became like actors in their lives, only playing a part. They had forgotten the art of being themselves. And the world lost much. When people lose sight of who they truly are, confusion and dissatisfaction set in, blinding them to love and all its simplicity.

As the kingdom steadily sank into darkness, more and more villagers became interested in finding cues and solutions to their dilemmas and undertook their pilgrimage to the temple.

One worried woman, dressed much better than the other pilgrims, made her way to the very front of the temple. The long, perilous hike to the temple had made her fearful. She longed to find answers that would calm her anxious heart. Winded and discouraged, she didn't want to miss a word of the priestess's wisdom. Her heart was heavy because her husband had lost his business when all the roads to Fataguro had collapsed in a terrible earthquake months before, and his saddlery no longer served the wealthy clientele in the surrounding kingdoms. Discouraged and desperate, the couple faced losing all that they held dear—their home, his business, and worst of all for the woman, many of her extravagant shoes. She wondered, *how do I keep loving him despite the loss?*

The priestess said:

"Some people think love is earned.

Just being is enough.

Love would never let itself by circumstance be spurned;

true love won't flee when things get tough,

nor let itself be lessened in the shadows of a loved one's flaws;

a flaw is but a window into unconditional love."

Amalthea never spoke long, but after she did her glow shone brighter and left the pilgrims in a bit of a trance. That is, it left most people in a trance.

"What does it mean to love unconditionally? Aren't there always conditions for love to exist?" the worried woman whispered.

"No idea," the woman next to her in the front row whispered back.

"Is that it? To love no matter what?" the worried woman asked, on the brink of homelessness, feeling the loss of her elegant shoes more deeply than before. A darkness crept over her spirit.

The worried woman shrugged her shoulders.

The priestess said:

"My light is your light. I can see your inner spark.

Let me rekindle your light through mine."

Other pilgrims shushed the doubters quickly, for it was terrible to miss a single word of Amalthea's philosophy. And they had all risked much to travel to the temple to find an end to their confusion. Among the crowd was a man who also thought he'd lost almost all hope and who made his way to the temple in search of his beloved wife. He believed that the priestess's wise words might inspire him to understand a woman better. You see, this man treasured knowledge the most, seeking it even at the expense of the ones he loved. And, slowly, in the smallest of ways, the wife and the man had become strangers. Eventually, his wife ran away in search of freedom and left her heartache behind. As the man sat in the glow of the priestess, he asked himself, *how do I keep loving her when she left me?*

The priestess said:

"Unconditional love has no boundaries.

Why do you expect or require?

Was she happy?

Let her freedom be your joy.

Let her happiness be your light."

"There must be more to this. Some riddle to solve or quest to complete?" the man asked.

The priestess said:

"My light sees you,

honoring your light from far away."

"I don't feel that I'm shining a light at all. I feel like my wife stole my light from me," he said.

The Priestess said:

"My light supports your light, wherever it may go."

The man was filled with a peace he didn't quite understand. Gone was the longing to know where his wife was and what she was doing. He left the temple pondering the simplicity of the idea that his light had never dimmed, instead of the confusion he suffered while trying to find his wife and being blind to the wisdom of just letting her go.

On his way out of the temple, he passed an old couple just outside of the golden temple doors. The old man held a cane as he walked through the golden doors, and he walked much slower than the rest of the pilgrims.

"The priestess isn't what I expected," the man confessed.

The couple paused.

"I expected her to answer my question, but she made me understand my wife's pain," the man said.

The couple nodded, a bit bewildered. The young man seemed to have a glow about him. The couple wished him well before they entered the temple. They found a place to sit on a beautiful marble bench.

The woman sighed. "I don't know where to begin," she said. "I don't know what question to ask."

"Just ask, my dear. The priestess will know what to do with your question," her husband said.

"Priestess . . ." the old woman began. She cleared her throat and tried again. "Priestess . . . our son has not talked to us in a long time because he is busy with his adult life. He won't reach out to us, even when we try to contact him. How do I stop this ache in my heart, as I deeply miss him?"

The priestess said:

"My light supports your light, wherever it may go."

The old man shuffled in his seat. "In a way, we have lost our son, like you lost your daughter. What is the secret to your happiness?"

The priestess said:

"I've lost my daughter only in an earthy way.

In spirit, she's always with me.

As my inner glow, she works with me by

teaching you the language of unconditional love.

For love is all that's good and right.

The light in her is now the light,

and when I teach love, the lesson you seek,

then her light burns brightly within me."

The old woman let out a sigh of relief as if the weight of every one of her son's unreturned messages had dropped off her tired shoulders.

"Man's inner flame always burns with the light of love,

within this temple, and within thy breast, one and the same.

If love that's unconditional is your quest,

just look inside yourself.

Your flame burns brightest and best."

Because the people of Fataguro had forgotten who they were, they became confused by Amalthea's simplicity. But in time, after hearing the priestess's message many, many times after many, many trips to the temple, the villagers lost their frustration over her confounding messages and saw her simplicity and clarity for what they were—unconditional love.

"You see, there is no secret; it's a very simple thing:

Love is simple, for there's nothing to construct.

It is the base of everything that's ever taken wing.

We all have it inside of us, where it is safely tucked."

AMORIS LINGUA

LOVE IS SIMPLE

YOU ARE IN EVERYTHING

No, You are Not only Just one Person Anymore,
Because You are in Everything.
I used to not Understand
And to Frantically search for your Smile,
For Your Voice and Laughter and Hugs,
For your Wit and Pensive Stares
While you were looking out, into that unknown
Expanse
That I couldn't Pinpoint or Jot Down.
Even amongst those Strangers Passing By,
I used to Frantically Search for a Glimpse of You
And Mistakenly Think that You Were just Playing
Games with Me,
Just like When you Were Little, When you would
Hide behind a Tree,
then Suddenly Appear with a Big Smile On,
Saying, "I Fooled you again, Mom."
And yet, no, Lengthy Days and Sleepless nights
Passed,
Without Receiving a Sign that you were Hiding,
Nor playing Games.

Those Days So Slowly turned into Weeks, and then
So Slowly into Months
And the Restless and Sleepless Nights became a
Time of Refuge
For all of my Thoughts, and Occasionally, Also for
my Dreams About You.
It is in that Unchanging Love of Mine Towards You
That I Now Realize that That's where I can Find You.
It is Not in People nor Crowds nor Places
It is Deep Down in My Heart and in the Realization
That Where there is Love there is Light and therefore
there is Life
That is where I can Find you,
Because You have never Ceased
But Only Transformed,
Back into that Light that Shines ardently all Over
the Valleys and the Mountains
and the Lakes,
That Light that Drives Out the Deep-Rooted
Darkness
Of this Amazing World, that So Needs Your Healing.
That is where I Find You,
In that Light that Shines its Love,
and which has always been at the
Very Core of My Being.

April 18, 2020
Santa Rosa Mountains, Southern California

THE MYSTICAL LAKE OF LOVING KINDNESS

nce upon a time, there were two elderly dogs, Peanut and Jones, who had always lived together in an old, battered crate at an animal farm on the outskirts of a sprawling city in the far, far East. Long ago, a well-meaning lady had found them on the street as puppies and dropped them both off at the animal farm. Many other dogs had been born or were taken there, but many were adopted by unscrupulous people who made the dogs fight each other in dog fighting rings. All of the animals had many scars on the inside and the outside from leading such miserable lives.

Peanut and Jones had spent their entire lives together, and although they weren't siblings, they felt like they belonged to each other, just like two brothers. They helped each other heal from the scars they had inside.

One day, a poor lady came by the animal farm. She lived by herself on a lake and she was very lonely, but she had always loved animals, especially dogs. Because she lived in a tiny house, she barely had enough room for one dog, so she had to make a tough decision. Would she pick Peanut or Jones? She took Jones home with her, only because Jones was the smaller of the two. It made her very sad to separate them, but she knew in her heart that one day she would come back and adopt Peanut too.

After she took Jones from the crate, Peanut became very sad. The separation made Jones very, very sad too, so much so that they both stopped eating and sleeping.

The Queen of the Fairies was alert that day and very sensitive to the sadness of animals. Drawn to the sadness between Peanut and Jones, she busily set out to see what she could do. The glow of loving kindness that emanated from the poor woman led the Queen of the Fairies to the animal farm. She overheard the poor woman's lament.

"I can't possibly take care of myself, let alone two animals. It wouldn't be fair to the poor things to starve to death. One day I'll return, after I've sewn enough royal clothes for the princes and princesses at the castle. Then I'll be back for you, Peanut."

This made the Queen of the Fairies unable to fly as high as before, because fairies need happiness to reach great heights and fly far afield. The Queen of the Fairies stayed with Peanut and tried to cheer him up as he watched his best friend leave with the poor woman. When the queen felt strong enough, she watched for the poor lady's glow in the night and flew to her humble abode, a room in a barn by a lake. There, the lady sat at her spinning wheel, creating the most incredible garments the Queen of the Fairies had ever seen. But the poor woman stopped spinning when she ran out of thread.

The woman bent over her spinning wheel and cried in the darkness as Jones slept in his straw bed. "How will I ever be able to save Peanut?"

The gaze in Peanut's eyes stayed with the poor woman. And the gaze in the poor woman's eyes stayed with Peanut. You see, the lady had the gift of tenderness, which left her eyes glowing in the most unusual way, certainly in a way Peanut had never seen before. The poor woman's loving kindness had led her to feed street dogs and puppies all her life. But she could not adopt any, because she was very poor and her home was very tiny. All the money that she made went to feed the strays. She only saved enough to eat bread and drink water.

The Queen of the Fairies waved her magic wand, which gave the poor woman an idea.

The poor woman picked up some straw from the floor of the barn and spun the straw into gold. At first the wheel appeared to just spin golden thread, then it turned into something more. The poor woman became so excited at her good fortune that she didn't want to stop spinning the straw, thinking she might lose the power to make the incredible thread. She spun day and night and finished weaving a dress with the golden thread, which to her surprise had a most unusual glow. It glowed with something much more precious than gold—the loving kindness of its maker.

When the princess received the dress with the golden thread and the inexplicable glow, all the other princesses in the kingdom wanted the poor woman to make their dresses too. Soon the poor woman couldn't make dresses fast enough to keep up with the demand.

Every time she got paid, she bought food for the dogs in the streets with her wages, took care of Jones in her teeny-tiny room in the barn, and only then did she think about spending any money on herself. Still, she couldn't get Peanut out of her mind. The last glance they shared still loomed large in her mind. She couldn't figure out what to do. She had the money now, but no room in her house.

Next to the poor woman's little house, there was a mystical lake called the Lake of Loving Kindness. The mystical lake could grant three wishes to those who showed up with true loving kindness in their hearts. The poor woman knew this, and therefore she had waited her entire lifetime for the right time to make her wishes. She knew her moment had come.

Because the mystical lake knew immediately if the person approaching had genuine loving kindness in their heart, as soon as it sensed the poor woman's approach, it asked, "Tell me, poor woman, how can I help you accomplish your three wishes?"

The poor woman knew from the bottom of her heart that she wanted a cheerful home for Peanut and Jones to live together, but she wasn't able to accommodate them because of a lack of space. She paused and thoughtfully considered her wish, as the moment only came once, and she didn't want to squander her opportunity.

She said, "Dear Mystical Lake, I would like to grant Peanut and Jones enough room in my house for them to roam freely, because cruel dog fighters have crated them all of their lives."

Waves rippled over the mystical lake for a moment or two, and then it said, "Good woman, I know that when you spin your straw, it turns into gold. With the gold that you make, why don't you buy yourself a bigger house?" Its words soothed the poor woman.

"Dear mystical lake, you see, with the money that I make, I buy food for the many strays in my village. I can't afford to buy myself a new house," the poor woman replied.

The mystical lake churned in a way that made the poor woman believe it was alive. Upon hearing such an example of loving kindness, the lake granted her wish in a way the woman never expected.

"Go now, your wish is my command," said the mystical lake.

"Thank you!" the poor woman said, not knowing how her wish would come to pass. But going on faith, she went back to the animal farm that same day and picked up Peanut. It was all she could do to not adopt every dog in that place. She didn't understand how people could be so cruel as to hurt animals for sport. This made her heart sad, and she hugged Peanut closer as she walked back to her tiny home.

But when she set foot on the teeny path that led to her tiny home, she discovered that her home had grown! It wasn't tiny at all! Peanut leapt out of the arms of the poor woman and jumped over the new white picket fence and ran to the front door. Jones hopped up to the window when he sensed the poor woman and Peanut at the front door.

"Peanut! Here is your beloved Jones!" The poor woman said when she opened the front door. "Jones, here is your special friend!"

The poor woman's heart grew in that instant, for it is well known that hearts get bigger and their capacity for love grows each time they show compassion.

Jones and Peanut ran outside and played. They chased after each other until they fell into a pile on the beautiful lawn, where there were many flower beds—because the mystical lake knew that smelling flowers was one of Peanut's favorite things to do.

The poor woman explored her beautiful new lakeside home. The mystical lake had placed everything in the home that she had ever wanted—a wraparound porch where she could rock in her rocking chair on endless summer nights and a kitchen big enough to cook for the Queen of England! And unbeknownst to the poor woman, the mystical lake had also included a gorgeous little rock garden so that the Queen of the Fairies would be able to visit in style and see what her gift had helped create.

While the poor woman admired her spacious new home, the mystical lake said, "Good woman, tell me, what is your second wish?"

The poor woman didn't need long to consider this time. "Dear Mystical Lake, I would like more straw to spin, so I can make more gold that I can sell. With that money, I can bring home, care for, and feed all the crated dogs at the animal farm."

A ripple of warmth rushed over her body like a waterfall. She instinctively descended the stairs to the beautiful basement, and just beyond the fully provisioned pantry, filled with rows and rows of canned jelly, jams, and summer vegetables, stood mounds of straw nearly filling the place up to the ceiling. She could barely find her spinning wheel!

As soon as the the no-longer poor woman started spinning, the big home filled up with lots and lots of gold, which helped Peanut and Jones play lots of great games of hide-and-seek. The Empress immediately bought all the gold, and the poor woman made so much money that she wasn't just able to rescue all the dogs at the animal farm, but was able to buy them all comfy, new beds and feed them the healthiest food. She had so much room left over that she brought home all the strays she met on the streets too, so Jones and Peanut had many new friends. There was an abundance of straw and gold and space and food for all, including for the woman, who, despite the abundance, still lived on only bread and water.

Again, as she went back to her new home, the mystical lake asked the woman, "Dear woman, what is your third and final wish?"

Since the poor woman's heart overflowed with joy, she couldn't think of another wish. She skipped down a beautiful path lined with white roses to the dock at the lakeside and replied, "I'm leaving the third wish to you, to grant abundance to another poor woman, just like you did with me."

The mystical lake gurgled its reply. "So let it be written. But tell me, why do you only eat bread and water when you could eat anything your heart desires?"

The poor woman replied, "No amount of money or riches could surpass the priceless joy I have in my heart, and no amount of money or riches could change my habits. I am a simple woman and enjoy a simple life. You've been so kind to show me pure joy. Thank you, gentle lake."

As the woman walked up the path to her new home, she opened her front door to find all the puppies and elderly dogs playing and sleeping. Just beyond the foyer in the large dining room, Naeltim, the sylph of the air, had arranged an amazing banquet on a large dining room table that sat below crystal chandeliers. The feast included every holiday favorite imaginable—a perfectly roasted turkey with all the fixings, succulent duck, a juicy beef tenderloin, the creamiest of mashed potatoes, the yummiest of gravies, the sweetest of strawberries, the most mouth-watering rhubarb and raspberry pie, and the best homemade dog biscuits cooked lovingly over an open fire—the third and final wish granted by the Mystical Lake of Loving Kindness.

LOVING KINDNESS

UNTITLED

Mom. She has blond hair,
she loves plants, and loves the air.
My mom is always on time,
and I don't know how to rhyme.
My mom loves shoes as much as I don't like to
lose.
My mom is pretty, and she lives in the city,
she is very smart and is getting a Ph.D. in art.
My mom loves to explore, however, she has a
tendency to snore,
she loves science, while Mrs. Koczan is part of the
same alliance.
My mom has a very high passion for fashion,
she is very optimistic which is an interesting
characteristic.
My mom is a fan of cheese,
and is an expertise at her ABCs.
My mom loves France, and her language skill is
very advanced.
She is tall while Johnny Depp is small.
My mom is an authentic photogenic.

Blaise, 9 years old

EPILOGUE

WHERE THERE IS LOVE, THERE CANNOT BE ANY FEAR

Emotion can sometimes overwhelm us, but it doesn't have to be that way. Getting in touch with our deepest feelings is an encouraging way of understanding ourselves better and of realizing that no matter what happens, we are always safe. It's a journey, down here on this beautiful planet Earth, and how about we start speaking from our spirit's infinite wisdom from now on and cast our fears aside, once and for all? Once we realize that everything has a spirit of its own and that everything is interconnected, how can we possibly be fearful? Spreading love and peace and hope is part of the healing process, and we all know that where there is love, there is also life, but also know that where there is love, there cannot be any fear.

WHAT DIFFERENCE DOES IT MAKE

What Difference Does It Make,
If You are here in the Flesh or in Spirit,
Knowing that You have always Existed, and
Always Will.
What Difference Does it Make,
Knowing that We have always Been Connected and
Always will Be,
in one Way, or the Other.
What Difference Does it Make,
Knowing That You have Now Transformed,
And that Here on Earth Your Light will Keep on
Shining
Upon those Who have Lost theirs.
I thank you For your Support,
I thank you For your Love,
And, especially, I thank you for your Light.

Your Mom in this Lifetime
Your Friend Forever

April 26, 2020
Cahuilla Tewanet Scenic Overlook,
San Bernardino National Forest, California

ACKNOWLEDGEMENTS

A special thanks to Laura Elliott, who helped me to transform the abstract thoughts in my head into physical form; my editor, Dakota Nyght; my assistant, Nancy Cavillones; Marit Cooper, my insightful illustrator, with whom I resonated right away; Emanuel von Malmborg, Altea Bianchi Bellfort, and Sabrina Quiroga, some of Blaise's amazing and sweet friends from around the world who helped me recollect other facets of Blaise's spirit; my son Shane, who has helped me stay grounded throughout the difficult process of healing; my friends Erika Mauro, Angela Crimi and Maria Sarro, my soul sister Cinzia Lanza and my soul brother Assefa Argachew; my brother Luca and my uncle Umberto and aunt Evelyn; Kari Halvorson, Lee Cook, Kathy Ganev Soto and Julie Cobb, whose spiritual guidance has been priceless; my numerous sponsored children, whose presence is invaluable; Steven Mulei, who makes me so proud to be his "mom"; my wonderful friend Gina Manola, whose life experiences have been so incredibly similar to mine and who understands what it means to lose a loved one to suicide; and, finally, my amazingly patient boyfriend Jon, who has been there for me through all the dramatic ups and downs, and whose constant love and grounding presence have helped me to slow down and stay in the moment. And last but not least, I want to thank my two little clowns, my dogs Piper and Peanie, who always make me smile. You two constantly teach me what unconditional love is.

BIO

LAURA FORMENTINI is an author, nonprofit photographer, and philanthropist. While working as an advocate to encourage people to travel, see more of the world, and catalyze positive global change, she became a child welfare activist and a supporter for the prevention of cruelty to animals. Her philanthropic work spans the globe, touching lives in Puerto Rico, Kenya, Malawi, Italy, and numerous countries in Asia.

Over the years, Laura has sponsored more than forty children through Plan International, an organization that advocates for children's rights and equality for girls. She is currently partnering with them to write a book revealing untold stories about the positive impacts of child sponsorship.

Laura is currently writing "Coming Home," a memoir about her time in Africa, and finding creative ways to travel safely as she continues to spread the message that practicing "Love in Action" not only brings healing to our personal lives, but holds the key to healing the world. She holds a Bachelor of Science in Archaeology and Art History from Washington University in St. Louis, Missouri, and has worked as an archaeologist in numerous European countries.

Twentyone Olive Trees: A Mother's Walk Through the Grief of Suicide to Hope and Healing marks Laura's debut as a novelist. She lives nomadically with her family.

For more about Laura, please visit
www.lauraformentini.com.